HOW TO GET A
JOB
IN A RECESSION

2012 edition

A COMPREHENSIVE GUIDE TO JOB HUNTING IN THE 21ST CENTURY, COMPLETE WITH MASSES OF FREE DOWNLOADABLE BONUSES

BY DENISE TAYLOR

Amazing People Est. 1998

Award Winning Career Coaching Company

Brook House Press
www.howtogetajobinarecession.com
simon@BrookHousePress.com

ISBN 978-0-9561755-1-9
Cover and Interior Design by Tudor Maier
Whilst the author has made every effort to provide accurate websites at the time of publication, the author does not assume any responsibility for errors or for changes that occur after publication.

Bonuses
For downloadable forms and audio visit
www.HowToGetAJobInARecession.com

By the same author
Now you've been shortlisted, Harriman House
Winning Interview Answers for First-time Job Hunters, Trotman Publishing

Acknowledgments

This book is dedicated to my clients, who enable me to do the work I love.

This book would have remained a task to do some day without Asif Hasan, Producer/Director with ITV who made the suggestion, more than once.

My thanks go to all the many clients I have worked with over the years who came to me unsure about how to get a job and left with increased confidence and a great future. I feel so blessed to have a job I love so much and the chance to work with so many fantastic people.

I'd particularly like to thank David Hebblethwaite, Mital Kinderkhedia, Richard Browning, Richard Lane and Steve Marsh for reading and commenting on my drafts and being fantastic clients.

I also wish to thank Malcolm Veitch for editorial support, his contribution has been invaluable.

Finally to thank my husband Simon and family who were patient with me whilst I withdrew from family life – a book takes so much more time than expected.

Denise Taylor
Tewkesbury, England
September 2011

Foreword

by Gladeana McMahon

It has always been the case that knowing how to find and secure the right position is a crucial skill. However, given the current economic climate and that which is likely to be with us for a few years yet, such skills need to be honed to a fine art. When Denise asked me to write a foreword for the second edition of her highly successful book I was delighted to do so. In this edition, she has taken what's good and made it even better ensuring the reader is helped every step of the way.

Although the current situation may make the process a little more challenging, what Denise has done is to demonstrate that it is possible to beat the recession with careful planning, thought and creative thinking.

The opportunities exist and it is a case of knowing how to find and make the most of such opportunities. There are ways to overcome the difficulties being faced and although no one will say it is easy, this book provides you with all the tools you need to present yourself effectively and well thereby increasing your chances of success.

Not only is Denise Taylor an expert in her field, but she has the knack of presenting the information and skills required to get the most from these challenging times in a logical and accessible format. She makes no assumptions about any pre-existing knowledge an individual may have and takes the reader through all the steps required to successfully deal with the various aspects of the job search process, such as designing a CV to practical interview skills. All the research available suggests that creating and using your personal and professional networks is a key to success and this book helps you tap into these to good effect. In addition, Denise is able to help the reader understand the job market, and brings together up-to-date information and the ways that creative thinking and commitment can get you what you want even in these challenging times.

A practical, down-to-earth, comprehensive and easy to read book that will help many people recognize that in every crisis, there is an opportunity if you only know how to go about finding it.

Gladeana McMahon FAC, FBACP, FIMS, FISMA, FRSA, is Chair of the Association for Coaching UK and Co-Director Centre for Coaching. She is listed as one of the UK's Top Ten Coaches by the *Independent on Sunday* and the *Sunday Observer* and a three time award winning coach.

Preface

This book is for you if you want to increase your chances of success in getting a job in challenging times. You may have been job hunting for some time and want to know why you are not getting shortlisted, or want to get ready in case you need to find a job quickly. This book will help you review what you have done and provide you with the tools you need and a plan to improve your strategy.

I'm Denise Taylor, a chartered psychologist and award-winning career coach. For over twenty years, I've been helping people identify their skills and what they have to offer a potential employer, working with them to identify a job they'll love, and supporting them in their job search.

I wrote the first edition of this book at the end of 2008, following my involvement with the ITV Tonight programme, *How Safe is Your Job?* I worked with people who had been unemployed for months, partly because they weren't realistic in their job aspirations, but also because their job search was not very effective.

This second edition was written in summer 2011; the situation has worsened, more people are being laid off in both the public and private sectors, and it remains challenging to get a job; fewer jobs being advertised, so the competition is tougher. Whilst the unemployment rate remains at a similar level to that of 2008 (approximately 7.8%), this takes no account of the number of people having to work in low-paid part-time jobs and those who choose not to register as unemployed. People wonder if they will ever get a job, but **opportunities are out there and you can get a job if you approach your job search as if it were a marketing campaign.**

There are significant changes between the first and second edition of this book. Most chapters have been extensively revised to take account of the most up-to-date techniques you can use, and new chapters focus on LinkedIn, on being found, and on research. Greater emphasis is placed on being proactive rather than on relying on the traditional way of applying for the jobs that are advertised.

Section 1 is focused on getting ready, creating a job search plan, getting organised, thinking about what you want to do, and considering the different ways to get a job. Section 2 is about getting the basics in place, compiling a CV, creating your personal message, getting started on LinkedIn.

Section 3 concerns finding things out, through networking, fact-finding interviews and research. Section 4 focuses on traditional job search, finding and replying to job ads, creating the cover letter, and using recruitment agencies. Then we get active in section 5 as we focus on the hidden job market, advanced LinkedIn and new approaches you can take. Once you get shortlisted, Section 6 will provide advice on selection, the interview, psychometric testing and assessment centres. Section 7 focuses on keeping going. It includes how to stay motivated, and what to consider before you say yes.

I've taken a multimedia approach to this edition. Access all the forms you need as complimentary downloads from the website, and download audio so you can listen to advice as you drive to interviews, go for a walk etc. You can also sign up for a 21-day eProgramme – each day you will receive an email guiding you on what to do that day.

You can access all downloads from this website: www.HowToGetAJobInARecession.com.

Wishing you all the best in your job search

Denise Taylor
Tewkesbury, England
September 2011
Denise@amazingpeople.co.uk

Contents

Section 5: Active Job Search

Section 6: Selection

Section 7: Keeping going

Introduction

This book will guide you through the different approaches needed to get shortlisted and then get the job offer. Too many people take a 'scatter gun' approach, sending out numerous CVs with general information not tailored to a specific position. It's much more effective to take a two-pronged approach, keep an eye on the jobs that are advertised but focus more on building connections, getting known and targeting companies directly.

In this second edition we will ensure that you have systems in place to make the traditional means of job search as smooth as possible so you can focus your energy and time on taking direct action. Finding a job is like selling a product: you need to understand the needs of the buyer (the hiring manager) and make sure that you provide what they seek. You also need to be found, and there are many ways to get your name out there. Uploading your CV to a job site is the least effective way of being found.

The world of work has changed. There are no longer careers for life, only a job for now. Sometimes a job doesn't even exist till you get in touch with a company. It's only when they see what someone has to offer, and that someone can demonstrate how they can meet the company's needs that a job is created.

I've written this book for you. Maybe you've lost your job to redundancy during these difficult times. Maybe you can't stand another day in the position you have now, or you've recently left college or university and don't know where to start, or your family commitments have changed and you are ready to enter or re-enter the job market.

Whatever the reason, you need help from a qualified professional. I'm sharing with you the techniques and advice I give to my clients; career coaching is my vocation and I've helped literally thousands of people identify what they want to do and achieve it. Kim had spent four months searching for a job and had not even got to interview, but within a week of my helping her, she was shortlisted for three jobs, and two interviews later she got a great offer. Lindsay was made redundant and was unsure about the proper way to apply for a new job. She followed the advice in this book and had a new job within weeks. Paul was unrealistic in his career expectations, and his CV and cover letter were too general and not targeted to the vacancy. Needless to say, he didn't find employment till he got focused.

I could fill this book with many more examples of client success stories; I have included some as appropriate. However, my main focus here is to provide practical help for you. Within these pages you'll go through the same process I use with my clients.

TAKING STOCK – HOW IS YOUR JOB SEARCH GOING?

If you have been looking for a job for some time you need to be honest, review your approach, see what is working and what needs to change. Too many people do the wrong things; they think that sat at their computer surfing on job search sites means they are actively searching. They think sending out 1000 CVs will help them get a job, but you **need to do much more than passively hitting apply on a website. You have to get out there, connecting with people and contacting companies directly.**

Many people think they are being proactive, but they are mail-shooting companies. You need to effectively research and target specific companies that need someone like you, so you can clearly focus on the benefits you offer to solve their problems.

GETTING A STEP AHEAD

Who could have predicted that Lehman Brothers would fall? But there were clues this was going to happen. The business press had written how Woolworths was finding it hard to keep its place in the current market. It had moved away from its core strengths of being a source for products of good value. There are steps you can take right now to get yourself ready for a job search in case your job becomes redundant. Get started right away and be ready to ramp up your campaign if you get notice of redundancy.

- **Network:** Stay in touch with people you know and develop relationships with others who may be able to help you in the future (or whom you may be able to help). Learn more about this in *Chapter 8 Networking*.

- **Skills audit:** Be clear on your strengths and what you have to offer. Don't rely on previous experience, but seek out training and other ways to keep your skills up to date and develop new ones. Your company may not pay for your training, but you could keep up to date through reading relevant articles and perhaps increasing your computer skills through practising at home. Read more in *Chapter 3, What do I want to do?*

- **Create an up-to-date CV:** Give it a critical review and make sure it includes up-to-date information. Read more in *Chapter 5, Creating Your CV.*

- **Review your finances:** Now is the time to review where your money goes and find ways to save. Reducing your debt or getting some savings together will take the pressure off you if your job is made redundant.

WILL IT BE ME OR YOU?

Often, it's not the whole company that closes, but just a percentage of staff that is let go (for example, one person in each store or department). So you need to look for ways to help increase the chances of your staying. Make sure that you do a good job so they are more likely to keep you.

- **Go beyond the minimum of what needs to be done,** and look for ways to add extra value, such as simplifying processes, improving customer service and reducing costs.

- **Be visible.** It's not just doing a good job but letting other people *know* you are doing a good job. Don't hide your achievements. It's also about being seen by senior staff, so get involved in meetings and focus groups; you want to be known to the key decision makers. Also get your boss to let their boss know what a good job you are doing.

- **Be indispensible.** Be willing to volunteer for the jobs others don't want to do and be flexible in helping out. Create great relationships with your customers or really learn the computer system. Your boss won't want to let you go.

- **Make or save the company time or money.** Look for what you can do to help the company's bottom line. Can you save them money? Simplify processes? Negotiate a better deal with suppliers?

- **Have a positive attitude.** When people are being made redundant, companies will often use this as an excuse to lay off the 'difficult ones'.

Be alert but don't worry. You should focus on doing a good job, not worrying about what might happen. But you can prepare your CV and be clear on the sort of work you would like to do should you find your job made redundant.

WHEN REDUNDANCY HAPPENS

You are highly likely to feel emotional, so take the time to express those feelings – it could be sadness, shock, disappointment, shame, resentment, and anger. You have every right to feel angry, especially if your employer has been reassuring you that all is OK. That's why you must look out for the signs of change in your company (recruitment freeze, loss of orders, sales people leaving).

You can certainly take time to grieve the loss of your job, but you need to let go fairly soon, otherwise you will drain your resources. It will be difficult to be successful in job search if you feel depressed or embarrassed by the redundancy. Look for ways to let those feelings out or they will fester inside you. Physical activity can help, so go to the gym, take a brisk walk, work in the garden or take a bike ride. You may also find it helpful to find someone to talk with.

DON'T TAKE IT PERSONALLY

Redundancy is more likely to be due to budget cuts and a lack of business than poor performance on your part. In this current recession, with an increasing number of people being made redundant, there will unfortunately be many other people in your position.

SO HOW DO I START?

People differ. Following redundancy, some people decide to take on any job that is offered, while others will hang on for the perfect job. But remember, 100% of something is better than 0% of nothing. Do your research, and if the likelihood of getting a similar job or your ideal job is remote, identify what jobs are more likely to use your skills and experience, and focus on them.

Waiting might bring you your ideal job, but waiting may also mean that you get into more debt. Think carefully about any opportunity. It might be something with less money, but it might also give you a chance to learn and develop, or get you into a company that may have other jobs advertised internally.

Short-term contracts may give you the chance to try out a different career or to build contacts within a company though a temporary role.

As you look at the available jobs, you might notice that they seek people with a certain skill set or experience. Could you use this free time to develop new skills?

Think carefully before deciding to sign up for an expensive course. Use fact-finding interviews to explore options and be very clear on the benefits before you spend your money.

THINK ABOUT WHAT YOU WANT TO DO IN THE SHORT AND MEDIUM TERM

Review your CV and think about what jobs are likely to become available. In the current economic climate, no matter how great you are as an estate agent or health administrator, if the jobs aren't available you need a new plan. You may need to take a job which pays a lot less than you are used to, but with the current economic climate, future employers (those you will approach) will probably prefer to see you have done something other than not working at all. The bigger danger when applying for a lower wage is in convincing people that you actually want the job and that you won't leave as soon as something better comes along. *Chapter Three, What Do I Want to Do?* will help you with this.

> To be successful in job search you need to have a plan and to follow it. This book provides the plan and teaches you what you need to do, but will you do what you know?

THINK ABOUT HOW YOU WILL SPEND YOUR DAY

When you were working, it gave you structure to your day, so how will you spend your time? If you want a new job, you must focus your efforts and devote your time to your job search. Look for jobs on line, but also be proactive. Get out and meet people, do research, get support from a career coach, engage friends and family – any and all of these things will help to speed up the process of getting a new job. The job search plan in Chapter 1 will help you to structure your day.

DON'T RETREAT

It can be easy to take a step back from the world and begin to get a bit too introspective. If you are feeling insecure or want to share your concerns, find someone to talk with. There's a tendency to become self-centred when we are unsure of the future. It's helpful to look for ways to be of help to others. Let your family know how you are and keep an eye out for them as well. Remember, family members may also feel stressed, wondering if all the bills are going to be paid.

BE AN ACTIVE JOB SEEKER

More people find jobs via the unadvertised job market than via the advertised one. You need to spend most of your time talking with people at meetings, events, and getting back in touch with people you already know. Specifically seek people you can talk with to find out more about jobs that interest you. As you get clearer on the job you want, the more others can help you in your job search. You'll read more on this in the Active Job Search section.

LOOK AFTER YOURSELF

Redundancy is stressful, and it will take a lot of energy and stamina to keep going. You will also want to make sure you are in good health for when you start your new job. So take some exercise, get out in the fresh air, eat healthy meals, and sleep well.

THINK ABOUT VOLUNTARY WORK

In the short term, you may have skills that a voluntary organisation could use. Volunteering gets you out of the house and adds some structure to your schedule (since you have to commit to a few hours each week). It allows you to meet others, some less fortunate than you, who may be able to help in your job search. It looks good on your CV as it shows you to be proactive and lets potential employers know that you didn't just sit back and wait for a new job, but used the time to benefit others.

Section 1
Getting Ready

Job search is a project and you need to be prepared. This section will help you to get organised, create a job search plan – with a downloadable file of forms to help you – be clear on what you want to do, and introduce you to different ways to get a job.

Chapter One

CREATING A JOB SEARCH PLAN

I want you to follow a structured and organised approach to your job search, to make best use of your time and keep you focused. You need to treat your job search like you would a marketing campaign where the product is you and everything you do gets you closer to your desired result, a job.

Each day you will undertake certain activities – it's important that you do these, and review your progress at the end of each day. It may take some time before you get a job offer, but as you complete each action you can celebrate a mini success; completing the tasks means you haven't just sat back and given up.

Daily tasks include a review. The review stage is important. If, when you talk with people, they aren't clear on what sort of job you are looking for, revise what you say. If you are not getting shortlisted, review your CV and the way you complete application forms. As part of your review you should ask yourself:

- Am I actually doing the steps I should do each day and not just reading what to do?

- Do I need to discuss my approach with a job search buddy or a job search coach?

It's not enough to just read this book, you need to do the activities and **keep** doing them. Even in a booming economy some people give up on looking for a new job because it's hard work. But if you are committed and follow the steps you will get there.

To be successful in job search you need to have a plan and to follow it. This book provides the plan; it teaches you what you need to do, but will you do what you know?

Kim, Lindsay, Steve, Richard and many more got job offers, but others take much longer. When I review what's going wrong I usually find a number of reasons – their CV needs a rewrite, they don't have a structure to the cover letter, they are sending out generic letters to jobs they are clearly unlikely to get, and take far too long to do anything. Many times they just give up; Julie sent out personalised letters to 7 vacancies but without a positive response she has let her job search lapse.

Just last week, Paul asked me to review his cover letter for a job. I gave comprehensive feedback, all explained in *Chapter 11, Find and Reply To Job Ads*, but his second attempt, which came a few days later, still didn't address the points in that chapter. Follow the steps and put your effort into the jobs you are a good match for rather than into a general application for many jobs.

You can sign up for 21 days of emails to keep you on track. My clients like these and tell me they are helpful, informative and fun. Some days you may not have the time to compete a task, so either catch up on the next day or slow down your approach. Other days you may find it easy to move ahead. Work at a 'stretch' pace; you can't afford to take too leisurely a journey if you want to find a job in a recession.

Expect there to be some setbacks, but if you continue to nudge ahead, you will get there.

IT'S GOING TO TAKE TIME

Please be realistic about how long your job search will take. It generally takes three months in a good economy from first looking to starting work in a new job. In a recession it could easily take twice this. It depends on the type of job you are seeking; the higher your salary requirement, the longer it is likely to take you. It's obviously easier (quicker) to get a lower-paid job as there are so many more of them. I've allocated you the first couple of weeks for preparation. It could take less if you are already 'job–search' ready and/or you are working full time on job search. That's why it's important to have an up-to-date CV should you need to get a job fast. Too many people think of job search as something that can be done in 2-3 hours a week, but if your time is as restricted as this you will have barely begun even after several months.

Keeping a daily log and monitoring your progress will help in your job search. Noting down what you have done each day, what you have learnt from it and what you are going to do next day will keep you on track.

HAVE YOU BEEN UNEMPLOYED FOR A LONG TIME?

Time to review your approach. If your house wasn't selling, you would probably take it off the market, and put it back on sale a few weeks later as a new property, with maybe some rooms repainted, decluttered and more 'kerb appeal'. Better to remove your CV from the different job boards, go through the activities in this book and start afresh in a few weeks. Think about what else you can add to your CV; volunteer to do the work you seek for a voluntary organisation. Look to what short courses could enhance your skills etc.

DAY 1: HOW ARE YOU FEELING?

It can be quite scary looking for a new job, particularly if it's a long time since you last looked for one or you have yet to get a first job.

You may have used words describing your concern over the future, and how you feel right now – angry, resentful, bitter etc. but also, whilst perhaps a bit concerned and unsure, you may be excited; this might be the prod you need to start working for yourself or to do something new.

> **ACTION**
>
> Take 5 minutes to make a note of how you are feeling right now.

Many of us are in jobs that we don't really like – we find them boring, we have a boss who creates too many problems, we don't feel we are paid enough for what we do. So, particularly if you have got a reasonable redundancy payout, this may give you the impetus to do something you actually want to do.

We can't ignore our feelings and of course it's ok to feel disappointed, concerned, etc. But to be successful in job search, we also need to set these feelings to one side, or they will keep popping up as we apply for jobs and at interview. Continuing to feel bitter about what's happened won't help us perform well, and an interviewer will pick up on negative feelings.

ACTION

List three things you are grateful for. You can then refer back to this when things appear difficult.

So aim to concentrate on the positive. You may have included your family, your health, friendships and your ability to learn new things. These positive things will help you as you progress in your job search.

PRACTICAL STEPS

You also need to take practical actions. If you are not in work, you need to get on with relevant activities each day. This includes spending a minimum of 4 hours a day (on average) with effective job search activity. Other things you could do during the remainder of the day include voluntary work, exercise (could be a brisk walk each day) and developing your skills, such as learning to use Excel.

You may need a reason to get out of bed each day, and if you are feeling a bit low and despondent, having a preset schedule will be helpful.

Offering your skills to a voluntary organisation for one day a week can allow you to have meaning and structure to a day, work in a team environment, use and develop skills, and will be useful to include on your CV and to discuss at interview. You won't have just sat back and waited for a job. You might make some useful contacts as well!

Richard told me about the transferable skills he gained from voluntary work with the Citizens Advice Bureau which he hadn't anticipated, such as how to understand a situation and clarify problems in a quick and timely manner, control and direct meetings yet be courteous and emphatic, and how to deliver unpopular news.

If you are unemployed, register at the job centre – you can do this online or by phoning 0800 055 66 88. When you call you will need to have your National Insurance number, and details of your rent/mortgage payments, employment history and savings. They will arrange for you to meet with an advisor and let you know if you are entitled to any financial assistance or free training programmes.

DAY 2: GETTING ORGANISED – READ CHAPTER 2

Systems! You may love them or hate them, but for job search you are going to need to be organised. I love systems and have created all the forms you are likely to need including forms to help you plan your day; this chapter also covers setting up a personal support system, getting references and more.

You can access all the forms and much more from:
www.HowToGetAJobInARecession.com

DAY 3: WHAT DO YOU WANT TO DO? – READ CHAPTER 3

It's not enough to want a new job. You need to be clear on the **specific** job you want so that you can market yourself properly. In today's chapter you can complete various exercises to get you focused on who you are and what you ideally want to do. You'll then do a reality check. It can help to come up with two jobs, your ideal and a job that will do in the short term, so you have money to pay the bills.

HAVING FUN

If you are out of work, treat job search like your full time job, but still make time for things you enjoy doing – music, reading, sport, and woodwork, whatever it may be. Ensure you take time to do something you will really enjoy each day.

Are you now clearer on what you want to do? If not you may want to stay longer on this step or get some external career coaching or guidance.

DAY 4: WHERE CAN YOU FIND A JOB – READ CHAPTER 4

You can find advertised jobs but you can also contact companies directly. There are other options such as part time work, freelancing, consultancy, developing a business idea. Don't be stuck thinking you have to find a job via an online website; there are alternatives.

DAY 5: CREATE YOUR CV – READ CHAPTER 5

Your CV is the foundation of your job search campaign. Whilst many jobs will involve completing an online form, your CV will mean you have most of the information you need for this, and lots of jobs actually want a CV. Follow this chapter for a step-by-step guide to creating your CV. Part 1 is about how to collect the information you need, and Part 2 is about how to put it together. The chapter is written like a coaching session with Denise, so you should find it easy to follow.

DAY 6: CREATE OR IMPROVE YOUR LINKEDIN PROFILE – READ CHAPTER 6

LinkedIn is a great way to keep in touch with business acquaintances and also for developing new contacts. It's a way of expanding your network to help with fact-finding interviews and to find out about possible opportunities, and you need to be on LinkedIn to be found by recruitment agencies. Chapter 6 talks you through how to create your LinkedIn profile.

DAY 7: RELAXATION DAY

It's not just about work, so take some time to spend with family, friends or pursue an interest, or just relax and enjoy being rather than doing. Remind yourself of what you have done this week, you have

- Got your paperwork together.
- Planned how you will spend your time.
- Got clear on what job(s) interest you.
- Created your CV and LinkedIn profile.

DAY 8: CREATE A PERSONAL MESSAGE – READ CHAPTER 7

Today you will read Chapter 7 and be clear on your message. This will mean that when you meet people and they ask you what you are looking for, you will have a great reply.

DAY 9: NETWORKING – READ CHAPTER 8

Many people get a job through networking, talking with people they know, and building relationships with people who may be able to help. This chapter talks you through how to develop your network and the steps you need to take when you meet someone.

DAY 10: FACT-FINDING INTERVIEWS – READ CHAPTER 9

To find out more about a particular job you can do fact-finding interviews, and this chapter tells you how. You probably won't start doing these today, but you will understand what you need to do and be ready to get started on them to help in your job search.

DAY 11: RESEARCH – READ CHAPTER 10

Research is needed at different stages of job search, from clarifying what job(s) you are going to apply for to research before an interview. This chapter provides excellent resources to help in all aspects of job search, including advanced Google techniques.

DAYS 12–14: TRADITIONAL JOB SEARCH – READ CHAPTERS 11–13

Today you will review how to find and reply to job ads using the guidance in Chapter 11. Chapter 12 talks you through how to create a cover letter, and Chapter 13 is about using recruitment agencies. You will register on sites and get ready to apply for jobs.

DAY 15: RELAXATION DAY

Follow the suggestions for Day 7 above and remind yourself of the progress you have made.

DAY 16: ACTIVE JOB SEARCH – READ CHAPTERS 14–16

This means researching and contacting companies directly. For many this is a new approach, so today you will read through what you need to do and then put what you learn into action on the following days.

From now on you need to create and follow a plan; you can also download this from the website.

DAILY TASKS

- Plan in advance what you will do each day – many of the tasks will be done every day.

- At the end of each day review your activity: what did you do, what has moved you forward on job search and what hasn't helped?

- Think about any task you didn't complete; what held you back?

TRADITIONAL JOB SEARCH

- Research jobs on websites and upload CV (and cover letter) as appropriate.

- Read professional journals (many are online) to identify jobs.

- If you are interested in retail, walk around to notice any jobs that might be advertised outside a store.

- Research to find out more about a company and industry.

- Write cover letters highly focused on a job.

ACTIVE JOB SEARCH

- Practise and use your 'personal message' by talking with people

- Go to LinkedIn – comment on a discussion, answer a question, find someone to connect with, get in touch with someone you know.

- Undertake fact-finding interviews.

- Knock on doors with copies of your CV.

- Arrange to contact companies directly.

LOOK AFTER YOURSELF

- Get some exercise each day.
- Eat healthily.

Once you have got into good habits on job search you can read through the section on selection, in particular the sections on the phone interview and interview preparation in Chapters 17 and 18. Once you get shortlisted you can read about the interview and psychometric testing and assessment centres in Chapters 19–21.

You may need help in staying motivated, so Chapter 22 will be a great read. And finally you will get a job offer, and when you do you want to make sure it's the right job for you; Chapter 23 addresses the areas to consider before you say yes.

Once you get a new job, go back to **all** the sites where you uploaded your CV and details and delete or deactivate them so you can no longer be contacted. You don't want your new boss thinking you are already looking for a new job. Also note which sites were most helpful for you and which CV was most effective as you may, unfortunately, be in this position again.

No job is for life, so remember the lessons learned from this and keep your CV up to date just in case.

All my very best in your job search success.

Visit the website to download the additional resources:
- *Extensive range of forms.*
- *Audio clips.*

Chapter Two

GETTING ORGANISED

Getting organised includes creating a filing system to manage papers and forms, both online and paper versions, and forms to manage the different tasks and paperwork. You will need to identify people who will provide references. Before that though, you need to make sure you have a high commitment to the task of finding work, and have a personal support system in place.

COMMITMENT TO THE TASK OF FINDING WORK

"When you look to a date in the future, remember: if you had started today, you would already have achieved success."

– Denise Taylor

Looking for a job is a full-time job. If you are out of work due to the recession, you can devote many hours a day to your search efforts. However, if you are in a full-time job, you are going to want to plan your time carefully so you have the time and energy to devote to this task. You must be sure to continue to work effectively in your job no matter how much you may not like the work you do. There will be plenty of other people eager to take your position, and if your boss thinks you are not really interested in it, then it could be you who is the one to lose their job.

How will you find the time to spend on job search? Could you stop watching as much TV or get up at least an hour earlier each day? How about working on weekends or taking a day's holiday to focus solely on your job search?

If you begin any task in a half-hearted way, you are unlikely to succeed. You will stumble and be hesitant at the first sign of difficulty, and that bold decision to get a new job will fade away. So for now, think about your level of commitment. Make a note of how committed you are to your job search. 10 means you are totally committed, and 1 means you are not at all committed:

$$1 \quad 2 \quad 3 \quad 4 \quad 5 \quad 6 \quad 7 \quad 8 \quad 9 \quad 10$$

With a level of commitment of 7 or below, you are unlikely to reach your goal of getting that great new job. If you find one excuse after another for not starting, it represents lack of commitment. There is also the danger of having too many other commitments and not enough time for your job search.

PLAN YOUR TIME

Have an established routine – make sure you do some work each day. If you are in full-time work, will you complete your job search and applications before or after work?

Make a note of how many hours you will spend on your job search each week. This needs to be a minimum of eight hours, and ideally more. If you have limited time available, decide whether to give up other commitments, or accept that your job search might take a year or more. You could divide this time into so many hours per day.

> I will spend ___ hours a week on job search.
>
> What is your commitment level?
>
> $$1 \quad 2 \quad 3 \quad 4 \quad 5 \quad 6 \quad 7 \quad 8 \quad 9 \quad 10$$

There's a form to help you which can be accessed via the website.

PERSONAL SUPPORT SYSTEM

Job hunting can be one of the most challenging activities of our lives. We are likely to experience rejection not only once, but again and again. In a recession, it's going to be even tougher with nine or more people for every job vacancy, so you need people and things to keep you motivated when you feel like giving up.

It's imperative to have support and motivation from others. Of course, you'll want your friends and family on your side, but what will you do if they aren't supportive and encouraging?

Knowing how to find support in difficult times means we have a plan ready when the need arises, but don't forget to support yourself from within. Most of your job hunting will be done alone.

Look at the list of supportive system activities below and make a note of those you might turn to when things get tough:

- Hard physical exercise
- Talking with a friend
- Yoga / meditation
- Relaxation exercises
- 'Treating' myself (e.g., buying a new shirt or book)
- Talking positively to myself
- Writing out a plan of action
- Writing down my feelings
- Involving myself in a hobby
- Enjoying outdoors and fresh air
- A change of scene
- Listening to music
- Going to the pub / club
- Reading fiction
- Reading a self-help book
- Finding time to reflect
- Work with a counsellor or coach

Make a note of your top three ways of dealing with the negative aspects and frustrations of looking for a job. Then find out more about your options so you can create a plan. For example, where can you learn yoga? Are you able to arrange regular meetings with someone to 'keep you going' during a difficult period? This is important because not only will you have positive activities, but a friend as well to help you get through the rough spots.

CREATE A FILING SYSTEM TO MANAGE PAPERS AND FORMS

You will need easy access to a number of documents. An early task will be to find a place to store the following:

1. Master copies of your CVs: You will need different versions of your CV for different applications – have both printed and electronic versions available. Keep a master copy of each so you can review for future applications. You may also want a copy handy for review when making phone calls.

2. Certificates, letters of recognition, etc.: You may need to let a future employer see your certificates and diplomas. You may also want to show letters of recognition from customers, so get them all ready now. **Action:** Find these now and get them in a display wallet so you can take them along to interview to support what you say.

3. Applications and cover letters: Each time you apply for a job, keep all the information together – the advert, additional information, a copy of the application form, CV version, etc. In addition to storing your letters and applications on your computer, have printed copies easily accessible. **Action:** Have some plastic wallets ready to file away your different applications.

4. Speculative approaches to organisations, consultancies and agencies: Detailed information of each company, letters sent, and next steps to take. **Action:** Use the forms to keep track of progress.

5. Diary or personal organiser: To keep track of your appointments. **Action:** Make sure you have a great method of keeping track, on paper or online, and one that's easy for you to keep updated; there's a form for this too!

6. Stationery: Not photocopying paper, but good quality 100 gsm paper with matching envelopes. **Action:** Buy some decent stationery soon. Having postage stamps on hand would also help.

7. To-do list: So you are clear on daily and weekly tasks. **Action:** Start a 'to do' list and review it each day; a copy is in the online form library.

8. Contact list: Details of whom you contacted, the reason for the contact and any follow-up action. **Action:** Get started on your contact list today.

FORMS NEEDED FOR AN EFFECTIVE, WELL-PLANNED JOB SEARCH

Having worked with hundreds of clients, I know the forms that will help you in your job search. Each is referred to in the relevant chapter and you can access them all from the website. They include:

1. Plan of action
2. Daily activity log
3. Daily plan
4. Daily tasks
5. Networking record sheet
6. Personal contacts action
7. Weekly targets
8. Weekly summary of job search
9. Weekly review
10. Response to job ads form
11. Response to adverts record sheet
12. Phone message form
13. Job advert summary
14. Direct approach follow up
15. Interview self debrief

> **ACTION**
>
> Download these now and set up a folder on your computer to keep these master copies.

JOB SEARCH: DAILY ACTIVITY LOG

- List the objectives for the start of each day and then make a note of how you use your time. A review will ensure you are making good use of time and not getting bogged down or distracted!

- Try to just do one thing at a time and follow it through.

- It can be most productive to do telephone calls in a block, perhaps calling at 10–11am or 2–3pm.

- As you plan your day, make sure to leave some time for the unexpected.

- Your activity log helps you recall what you have done, whom you have contacted, and makes sure you follow through on each activity.

- List every activity you do alongside your comments on how well you are doing.

- Record information about the people you meet. Make sure you have their contact details correct. You may need to follow up on what they agree to do.

- Note names of any secretaries or assistants you speak with – they can be flattered that you remember their name.

Don't forget to include lunch breaks and relaxation.

EXAMPLE OF A DAILY ACTIVITY LOG:

13th February

I collected a national paper to scan for any jobs. I put a cross through those that were clearly unsuitable and used my highlighter to ring any that would be of interest.

Visit to library to read Financial Times to keep up on industry changes.

Chatted to another job hunter and went for a coffee. We swapped cards and will meet in the library next week to pass on any useful information. Glad I have her email details.

Saw that XXX services are expanding. They may have some upcoming vacancies in my area of expertise, I've noted to follow up.

Spent all afternoon on my application form to ABC Ltd, it was a complicated form so I was glad I had photocopied it yesterday so I could use it to create a draft copy.

Looked at my letter and tweaked it so I could send it to XXX. I rang first to find out who was going to be the most appropriate person to send it to.

Received a phone call from Colin Pemberton (01684 XXXXXX). He is a friend of Andrew Wilson and said there may be something coming up and he would like to meet. We have arranged to meet at the Old Swan, Cirencester at 11.45 this Friday. Forgot to ask for some info on the company but have noted to do an Internet search.

Made a note to follow up on the 10 letters I sent out last week, this will be my first task of the morning.

DAILY REVIEW

Complete each day with a review

- What did I do today?

- What was helpful?

- What hindered?

- What one action can I take tomorrow to make a big difference to help me reach my objective of a new job?

REFERENCES

Who to choose?

You will want to choose people who know you. Often you are asked for both work and personal referees. It's a good idea not to choose relatives because they don't carry much authority. Ideally, choose people who are professionals with a good reputation. Former employers carry the most weight, also key suppliers and customers who can vouch for the work you do. Referees are sometimes phoned and if they can clearly give examples of your achievements, it will definitely improve your chances.

Get their permission

Ask general permission before you start your job hunt. You don't need to contact them each time, but you may want to remind them you are still looking if your job search drags on. By asking permission, you show respect for them and their busy schedules. Not everyone will agree. Respect their wishes; a half-hearted testimonial is worse than no reference at all!

Letters of recommendation

It might be helpful to get a letter of recommendation that you can show when you go to interview, and that you can use excerpts of in your CV.

Brief them

Do they know what you have been doing in your current and previous jobs? Do they know what you are applying for? It can help to let them have a copy of your CV plus details on the job(s) you are applying for. Give each referee a copy of the CV and cover letter that you sent to the employer. Also, supply each referee with a copy of the description of the job you are applying for and a list of the specific features you would like them to mention to the employer. Make it easy for the referee to help you.

Have correct contact information

Make sure you have all details correct, especially phone numbers and email address. Also be sure you have their correct job title. It may have changed since you were last in touch. It's more official to include the person's work rather than home contact details.

Keep them informed

When you know that a referee has been contacted, give them a call to say thank you. Later, let them know if you did or didn't get the job. Periodically during your career search, send a letter of thanks to your referees, along with an update of how your career search is going. Developing your relationship with them can only enhance what they write about you. This will be a positive reinforcement of your interpersonal skills.

Remember to thank them

ACTION

Decide who will make your best references and get in touch.

When you finally get the job, you can let your referees know how much you appreciated their involvement. This will help them feel good about themselves and make them more likely to help others in the future.

Visit the website to download the additional resources:
- *Many forms are available to help you keep organised.*

Chapter Three

WHAT DO I WANT TO DO?

To some this may seem like a silly question. You bought this book because you want to get a job, but what job exactly? In a recession, not all jobs are attainable. Even worse, many are eliminated. Marie was expecting to get promoted to Land Director, but instead was made redundant when the building company she worked for lost 90% of its value. Kim was made redundant as fewer people were buying houses and she was no longer needed as a legal executive. Roger was made redundant as a sales manager for a car dealership when car sales dropped. They all loved their jobs and wouldn't have sought a change in position, but their redundancy gave them time to reflect on what they actually wanted to do. Roger was a natural sales person with an excellent track record and found a job quickly, but Marie and Kim took time to consider alternatives and take a fresh look at the job market.

Marie was able to refocus and adjust her skill set and is now working as a project manager in sustainable development. It doesn't pay as much as she earned before but she has a better quality of life.

Kim looked for work that would make good use of her high level of organisational skills and her legal background. She was fortunate to get two job offers and gained employment making great use of her particular skills and background. Her new job allows her to meet staff from law firms, enabling her to build contacts in case she wants to make a change when the economic climate improves.

Roger used the proactive approach and took another sales position, earning even more than before. Kim found her job in the newspaper and Marie was approached after uploading her CV onto a jobs site.

In a recession, the job you are qualified to do may not be available, so you may not be able to stay on the same career path – no matter how good you are. So you need to think about what else you **can** and **want** to do, to refocus skills to suit something else. If you have (or had) a job you hated, this might be the best time to consider doing something different.

Now it's even more important to be clear on what you want to do. Knowing yourself, knowing more about the job you seek, and being clear about how you match up will dramatically increase your chance of success. If not you will be one of the many who browse through job sites in the hope that something appeals. You must know what you are looking for; it makes it much easier when you meet with people, as you are clear on what you want to do and can clearly state what you seek. This applies when meeting people both in person and on LinkedIn etc.

> Being clear about who you are and what you want to do means that all your marketing material – CV, Cover letter, LinkedIn profile – send out the same message. You need to be consistent; everything must have a similar message to increase your chance of getting what you want.

MAKING A CHOICE – WHAT DO I WANT TO DO?

You have a choice: to look for something similar to what you have previously done or to do something new, but what?

You will be revising your CV so prepare by doing some analysis.

SKILLS

Firstly, what do you do well? What are the top skills you have? What are the tasks that you are praised for achieving, and what are you qualified to do? It's not just about what you have done in your last job; skills can include things you do outside of your main paid work such as a hobby or interest. That's what led Bruno to follow his dream of becoming a golf pro.

Skills are the things we have learned to do. We gain skills through both paid and unpaid activities. As you think about your skills, don't just think about the work you do in your day job. You may have gained relevant skills via hobbies (organised a wedding, or a group holiday) or perhaps voluntary work (leader of the Brownies). Perhaps you have entrepreneurial skills and have been selling things online or via market stalls.

Samira said: "*My top skills are paying attention to detail, being quick and accurate with numbers and being organised. I've got good listening skills and I'm the sort of person that others confide in, I'm creative and like developing new solutions.*"

Activity: Make a note of your top skills, if you need help, download the skills exercise from the website.

Some of these skills you will want to keep on using, but there will be many that you don't enjoy, so cross them out! With the ones that remain, make sure you are specific.

For example, which are better, your written or verbal communication skills? Are your verbal skills better in one-to-one situations or in large groups? Providing an example of this skill will be very useful for revising your CV and at interview.

Organisation: *I can organise people, information and events. For example, I planned a conference entertainment programme, negotiated with suppliers and produced publicity materials.* (This can then lead to a separate heading of 'Communication'.)

Identifying your skills reveals all you can do, and editing them determines which truly interest you. Doing this not only keeps you from focusing solely on using the skills you have, but shows you which skills you truly enjoy using.

> **ACTION**
>
> Provide specific examples of your top skills.

ABILITIES

"*Our abilities are perhaps the most fundamental piece of the career puzzle.*"

- Hutchinson and McDonald

Do you know your natural talents? You may be an accomplished musician, athlete, or artist, but it's likely your abilities go much further. Ability testing defines your natural abilities based on timed work samples, and covers a

ACTION

List your key abilities and strengths.

wide range of abilities including problem solving, spatial relations, verbal memory, observation, idea productivity and visual speed and accuracy. If you want to invest in an accurate assessment you could take the Highlands Ability Battery. Read more online. An alternative is to think about what you do and list your strengths and skills. It's important to ask others to help you with this as they may see hidden talents in you that you are not aware of.

INTERESTS

You may be great at a whole range of tasks but absolutely loathe the work; perhaps the attention to detail required in analytical work does not play to your strengths, and you want to be able to use your idea generation skills. Make a note of everything you enjoy doing. This does not need to be focused purely on work tasks; thinking more broadly can generate possibilities.

ACTION

Make a note of your top interests.

Even if you can't directly use your interest in a specific job, they can help with the work setting. For example, if you have a love of art and are an accountant, you could seek opportunities within art galleries, museums etc.

HAVE A CLEAR VISION OF YOUR FUTURE WORK ENVIRONMENT

Think about your ideal working environment. What sort of environment would enable you to work at your best? This includes the company, culture, salary, location and anything else you can think of.

Consider the size of organisation. For example, you could be a catering supervisor in a large company and move to be a catering manager in a smaller company. Or be a general manager in a smaller company and change to an operations manager in a medium-size company, etc.

If your travel-to-work distance is 30 minutes, it may seriously constrain your search, so could you extend it to a 90-minute journey? If you have constraints then narrow your search; there's no point getting excited if you see an ideal job and then realise it's 100 miles from your home.

HOW WOULD YOU DESCRIBE YOUR PERSONAL STYLE?

The following questions can help you understand yourself. For a more in-depth understanding, you will want to use a personality measure such as the Myers Briggs Type Indicator. Read more online.

- Think about when you are being positive. How would you describe yourself?

- Think about when you are being negative. How would you describe yourself?

- Think about when you've been in a difficult situation at work; how was it resolved and what was your part in this?

EXAMPLE: SAMIRA

Samira was made redundant from her job as a financial analyst. She was also a fully qualified accountant. She was concerned over being made redundant from a high paid job but had been working on a product she didn't believe in, with a not very supportive manager, and working for a large city firm with a long daily commute which didn't give her time for any other interests. By the time she got home from work each day she was ready to just slump in front of the TV. Her ideal working day would be working within a 30-minute journey from home and with the freedom to work from home at least one day a week. She was willing to earn less if it meant she could work with a company she believed in. Employment as an accountant in the charity sector would match many of her needs.

Write down the keywords that describe you, and then ask close friends or relatives to see if they agree. For each word, give an example of when you used your strengths in a positive way. For example:

- *Cooperative: I work well with other people. For example, my colleague had a problem with a project and several things needed completing at short notice. I reprioritised what I was doing to help her out, including staying late so that she met her deadline.*

- *Customer focused: I pride myself on doing all I can to achieve customer satisfaction. When I overheard a customer complaining at a till, I took them to one side (so it did not impact on other customers), listened to their problems and dealt with the situation swiftly. This resulted in a letter of thanks to my manager, and a larger order from the customer.*

Your responses can help in thinking about the role you want to undertake with a company and how you can best relate to others.

Samira said: *"I'm quite an outgoing person who has been forced to work alone for so much of the time. I'm assertive and not afraid to stand up for things I believe in. I am trusting and wonder if at times I can be a bit too trusting. I love change and am not constrained by traditional ways of working. I'm a perfectionist so I do a really good job but it does mean I can be a bit critical of others. I sometimes find it hard to meet deadlines as I can get distracted by other people."*

ACTION

List your top personal characteristics.

KNOW YOUR VALUES

When we live a life in line with our values, we concentrate on what is most important to us. This helps in decision making. For example, if health is our number-one priority, it will affect what we eat, how much we exercise and how we spend our leisure time. When we do work that is in line with our values, it is more of a calling than a job. When our values are incongruent with our career, it can lead to stress, discomfort and unhappiness.

My clients work through a values card sort exercise to help them decide between options; they compare shortlisted jobs against their top values. As you move towards your next job, making a choice that does not conflict with your personal values will ensure you are less stressed and more contented. You can identify your values by using a pack of values cards from my website, or use the list of values you can access from *www.stevepavlina. com/articles/list-of-values.htm.*

You need to identify 5–7 top values to aid decision making. When you look at your list, you may see there is some conflict. If both family and success at work are important to you, what will you do when you get offered a promotion that means working much longer hours? Or you have to travel a lot?

Make a note of your top values.	**ACTION**

PUTTING THIS TOGETHER

Summarise your answers to all the action steps and use this information to identify potential careers. There is a form to help you on the website. If you are not sure ask people you know or work with a career coach.

As you discuss this with others, make sure to tell them that you don't want advice, but rather their creative input.

Can you now draw up an ideal job description, outlining what it is that you want to spend your day doing? Also, give thought to what would be the ideal industry or sector for you. A particular job from Accountant to Writer can differ depending on whether you work in manufacturing, charity sector, high tech or education, etc.

Is the job available?

You have to be realistic, are there jobs available and how likely are you to get one? In times of recession, jobs that are still available include working in the energy industry, teaching, health care and care for the elderly. Children will still need to go to school, people get ill, and with an aging population there are likely to be more jobs available in the care sector.

It's worth keeping abreast of the news to see where the government is likely to invest money. For example, with investment in construction or green energy, these are areas you may like to consider. Companies may be cutting back on training and possibly advertising, but certain back-room functions stay in demand, such as IT and Finance. It could be worth looking into what you need to do to become a credible candidate in these areas.

Looking online

You can now find out more about these different jobs via my two favourite web sites. I've shortened the links to help you get to the right page, and you can also access these from the website.

http://bit.ly/profile4   *http://bit.ly/jobideas*

Both sites have links to job categories such as 'administration and clerical' or 'medical technology.' You can also use the search box to type in the name of a job that interests you.

Read up on job profiles when you want to find out if a job interests you, if you match the criteria needed, and if the pay scale and prospects meet your needs.

From this you can decide that a type of job is worth applying for or that you need to gain experience/qualifications before you are likely to be successful. Each site provides links so you can find out more. For example, if you are interested in being an events manager, you can follow up with seven organisations including:

- Association of British Professional Conference Organizers (ABPCO)
- Association for Conferences and Events (ACE) and
- Association of Exhibition Organisers, with details provided.

The sites also suggest similar jobs, for example:

- Wedding Planner
- Charity Fundraiser
- Marketing Manager
- Conference and Exhibition Organiser

These web sites are very informative and provide plenty of detail on what the job involves including common salaries and tips on how to find out even more details. Review your options and produce a shortlist.

MAKING A DECISION

List the jobs and compare them against your values, ideal work environment etc. You should then be able to prioritise them. It's now time for a reality check. You may find that the jobs which suit your interests and personality need different skills and experience from those you have gained in previous work, thus a radical change of career may be unlikely. In the current economic climate you may need to focus on what you are likely to get in the short term.

WHAT ARE YOU GOING TO LOOK FOR?

It may be a specific job, or it may be a broader area, but the clearer you are on the sort of job you want, the easier it will be when other people ask you what you are looking for. So write it down.

Does this answer the question of the type of job you are seeking, the sort of company etc? Read it out loud and fine-tune it till it sounds natural. You will find more detail on how to be clear on what you want in *Chapter Seven, Creating your message.*

WHEN YOU STILL DON'T KNOW

Many people need more extensive help in making a career choice, such as that provided by a registered guidance practitioner, chartered psychologist or career coach.

For many, the use of assessments can be highly valuable. As a chartered psychologist I am an expert in many of the most useful career assessments including the Highlands Ability Battery, Myers Briggs Type Indicator, Strong Interest Inventory, Birkman method and more. Access more details from the website.

Visit the website to download the additional resources:

- Skills Exercise.
- Read more about different assessments – Highlands Ability Battery, Myers, Briggs Type Indicator, Strong Interest Inventory and more.
- Web links.

Chapter Four

DIFFERENT WAYS TO GET A JOB

There are a number of ways to get a job. Most people put the greatest effort into searching for jobs they see advertised, either in newspapers or on job sites. But this can be the least effective method of finding employment. The problem with concentrating on jobs that are advertised is it's what everyone else is doing. Companies get swamped with applications and it's very difficult to stand out from the other applicants.

HOW DO COMPANIES FILL JOB VACANCIES?

First of all, they look within their company, and then they ask their professional contacts. If they don't find someone, they will eventually advertise the job in the press, contact a recruitment agency, or post the job on a professional association website. People talk about the hidden job market, but jobs aren't hidden, they just haven't been advertised yet. Contact a company at the right time and you could be on a shortlist of one.

You must, of course, still look at the advertised jobs, but this is just one option.

TRADITIONAL JOB SEARCH – THE ADVERTISED ROUTE (VIA PRINT AND ONLINE)

It's easy to see the jobs but

- The competition is high – companies get hundreds of CVs.

- You need to watch out for fake job postings. Some advertised jobs don't exist, because they have already been filled, the company may just be testing the water to see if there are any applicants, or an agency may be collecting CVs.

47

- Take care about how much personal information you include; you need to be mindful of identity fraud.

- You can find yourself approached by companies who want to sell you expensive programmes or get you to sign up for commission-only roles.

- You can get sucked into spending hours online. Limit yourself to a maximum amount of time each day.

TO INCREASE YOUR CHANCE OF SUCCESS

- Identify the most relevant websites and papers to research and read. Professional journals will often have jobs available on their website in advance of the print publication.

- It's easy to waste a lot of time on these sites, so research which sites are most appropriate for you and concentrate your time on those.

- Don't just approach the large sites. It's expensive for a company to post on them. Smaller companies will often use more niche sites.

- A keyword search will be used, so include as many keywords as possible.

- Be selective and spend time on the closest matches of your skills to the position, rather than sending unfocused letters to many.

- Carefully read the ad and ensure your letter and CV closely match their requirements.

- Respond promptly and log the date so you can follow up. Jobs may be removed before the closing date if the company is swamped with applicants.

- If you get a reject/regret letter, ask for feedback. Most of the time you won't get it, but occasionally you'll get a reply that will help with future applications.

RECRUITMENT COMPANIES

How to increase your chance of success

- It's imperative to build a good working relationship with your consultant so they will work for you. Don't hassle them but make sure you stay in touch.

- You can do a direct marketing approach to selected recruiters, clearly spelling out your strengths and what you are seeking.

THE HIDDEN JOB MARKET

We'll cover this in depth in Section 5. This is the most common way that people find jobs, but an approach that many use ineffectively. When you get in touch, a company may or may not have a job vacancy, but companies are always on the lookout for stars and you just might be the one!

How to increase your chance of success

- Networking will help you to find out more about the job and other job possibilities; look for ways you can help others, then they will be more likely to help you.

- Be on the look out for problems you can help an organisation solve. You can identify these via news reports in the press.

- Write a targeted letter and follow up.

- Research companies to approach by using a business library and online research methods.

- Find details of smaller companies in your chosen area through your local chamber of commerce.

NETWORKING

How to increase your chance of success

- Let people know what you are looking for.

- Look for ways to help them, either now or in the future

- Don't forget online networking such as using LinkedIn.

- Clearly identify your contacts and prioritise the people you will approach first.

- Document the results of your meeting; be polite and thank people for their help.

- Ask for more referrals.

- Keep people informed on how you are getting on.

SELF-EMPLOYMENT

Do you have the personal qualities to set up your own business? It's best to first talk to a career coach, especially if you are considering going into business for the first time. If you want to pursue this further you can get helpful advice from Business Link: ***www.businesslink.gov.uk.***

CONSULTANCY/ FREELANCE WORK

If you are able to get some consultancy work or a short term assignment, it might lead to a new career. Professionals may be able to get occasional work as holiday cover, or be called upon for peaks of work. When I started working for myself, before I started gaining clients I was doing freelance work with a number of different firms. Two days a month with a couple of different companies was quite lucrative. As I was developing my own business I had the flexibility to cover at short notice. Could you offer your services to local companies? Think about how you could help small businesses, perhaps.

There are many sites where you can sell your services on an ad hoc basis, such as www.elance.com, www.ifreelance.com, and www.odesk.com.

VOLUNTARY WORK

You probably don't want to work for free, but offering your services to a charity, can help you develop skills, remain active, meet people and demonstrate your energy, humanity, and 'can do' attitude to any and all potential employers. It's also a great way of developing skills to help you move into a new area. You also get to meet a range of people, thus extending your network.

Voluntary work can also be at a professional level. If you are an unemployed communications executive or business analyst, could you use these skills within a not-for-profit organisation?

As I mentioned earlier, Richard unexpectedly gained transferable skills from voluntary work with the Citizens Advice Bureau, concerning dealing with and solving people's problems quickly and effectively.

INTERNSHIPS

Many companies offer unpaid internships, but some are paid! Internships can work if you have clear objectives, and you get to gain experience that will enhance your CV and collect some LinkedIn recommendations as well.

MULTIPLE OPTIONS

Instead of thinking of just one job, you could aim for two or three part-time jobs. This would mean that you have some income as you start each job, and would increase your feeling of career security. Or you could seek out a part-time job alongside part-time study to learn new skills or update current ones. There's always a possibility of losing one job but not all three. It also gives you a chance to impress a future employer and to network within a new company.

You can combine two or more together. For example, you could seek out two part time jobs or one part-time job alongside self-employment. You don't have to wait for the perfect job; a part time or temporary job could be the right option for now.

Section 2

First Steps of Job Search

Now you know what you want to do you can create your CV, create an effective LinkedIn profile, and be clear on the message you want to communicate to others. This section provides effective and easy-to-follow guidance to get started on your job search.

Chapter Five

CREATING YOUR CV

INTRODUCTION

When I work with a new client, one of the first things I do is review their CV. Unfortunately, I see too many CVs that are ineffective, even those written or reviewed by people who claim they are experts.

There are many books on the market focused solely on writing a CV, so to cover this topic in one chapter is encouraging me to be succinct, just as your CV needs to be!

Your CV is a key element of your job search. You will use it not only for job applications but also for speculative enquiries. One version is not enough. It's best if your CV is tailored specifically for each job (or type of job) you apply for. This chapter will help you prepare the most effective CV possible to make your job search a successful one.

Generally, CVs will be up to two sides in length, and every statement on the CV must be relevant. You don't need to include everything, but it should highlight your achievements, skills and what you have to offer. If it gets you to interview, it has done its job well.

Many CVs have a poor appearance. They are too lengthy, have too many typos, or have a layout that is hard to follow. There are many different layouts used and I tend to use different styles to suit different jobs and individuals.

Font and layout can be left to personal choice although I suggest avoiding the templates found in word processing packages as they will make your CV look too rudimentary and it will stand out for all the wrong reasons.

HOW TO HELP THE RECRUITER

Less than a minute is spent short-listing each CV, so you need to highlight the key points, through layout, judicious use of bold and underlining, and careful use of white space. The goal is to get your CV in the pile that gets a second review.

IT'S HARD WORK BUT WORTH IT!

You can easily spend £300 or more on getting your CV professionally created, and for many, it's money well spent. To do it yourself, you will need to invest time in collecting the information you need, then in writing it as clearly and effectively as possible. The applicants that get shortlisted are those with CVs that are effective and focused on the job.

WHAT TYPE OF CV WILL YOU USE?

The three main categories of CV are:

- Chronological
- Skills-based
- Combination

The Chronological CV

The chronological CV is most effective for individuals who have a steady record of employment in an industry or functional area and want to stay in the same line of work.

It is not recommended when:

- You are changing careers or have changed employers frequently.

- You want to de-emphasise age.

- You have been absent from the job market for some time.

The Skills-based CV

Choose a skills-based CV if you want your next job to be in an area where you will have a significant shift in responsibilities, or to move to a different sector. Highlight skills and achievements rather than the chronology of events. A skills-based CV is useful when you:

- Are making a career transition.

- Want to return to a professional area you worked in earlier in your career.

- Want to disguise a previous career path.

- Have large time gaps in your CV and/or other biographical materials.

- Have extensive accomplishments in volunteer work or hobbies.

For example, John worked for many years as a church minister but wanted to pursue a career into human resources. Rosie had been on a career break for several years and needed a way of including all the skills and experience she had gained via voluntary activities. For both John and Rosie, a skills-based CV significantly increased the number of interviews they gained.

Why you need a skills-based CV

Too many potentially suitable applicants fail to get short listed due to the fact that they do not fit the expected applicant profile. A skills-based CV can help you to overcome this problem. Most of the first page lists relevant examples under the key requirements of the job, thus making it easy for someone to see how you will match up.

PREPARATION PHASE

Before you decorate a room, you get the walls and paintwork prepared and make sure the brushes are clean. When producing your CV, take the same approach; you will make faster progress if you collect all the details in advance.

STEP 1: WORK HISTORY

The first task is to collect the details on each of the jobs you have had so far. If your work history goes beyond 15 years, you may not need to go further back, unless there is something relevant to the current job you are applying for. For example, Kim was a legal secretary before following a career in hotel and catering. When she decided to apply for work as a legal executive, her previous work experience was relevant, despite its covering 20 years.

If you are a recent graduate, you need to ensure that you include details of all your part time work, and perhaps also include details of your other interests (passions, hobbies, voluntary activities) particularly if they reflect attributes such as leadership and organisational skills.

You may not be using all of this information in your CV, but it will be useful to be able to refer to it in the future. Sometimes when you complete an application form, further information is requested, and it's helpful to have the details to hand.

Don't forget about volunteer work. It can be relevant to include, for example, coaching a junior football team if you are seeking a teaching job. It will have more impact if it appears here rather than under Personal Interests.

For each job, make a note of:

- Dates (including month and year).

- Organisation name.

- Address.

- Job title.

- Brief description of the organisation.

- Your department's purpose and objectives.

- Main responsibilities. Include numbers of people managed and size of budget where appropriate.

- List your achievements - quantify wherever possible.

- What strengths/skills or attributes do these achievements reveal?

- What do you most enjoy about your job?

- What do you least enjoy?

- Why are you leaving?

- Who will give you a reference?

- Leaving salary and benefits

This may seem like a lot of extra work, but the aim of your CV is to get you to interview, and the thinking and reflection required to answer these questions will enhance your performance at interview.

STEP 2: EDUCATION AND SHORT COURSES

Think back over each job and make a note of all courses, both internal and external, which you have completed. Some employers will ask to see your certificates, so find them and put them in a folder. Don't be tempted to fabricate your results. If you are found out, you will likely be dismissed.

For each course, make a note of:

- Title of course.

- Date of course.

- Length of training course.

- Training provider.

- Benefits gained.

Computer Experience

Almost all employers want people who are comfortable using a word processing package, email, etc. How confident and competent are you? Make a note of the software you can use, and for each, list:

1. Frequency.

2. Examples of use.

3. Level of comfort in using it.

Languages

Make a note of any languages you can speak and the level of fluency, e.g., French (fluent); German (basic). Don't fib! I've interviewed someone who said they could speak Polish, but was unable to answer a simple question. As recruiters we think that if they have fibbed here, where else might they have done so?

STEP 3: PERSONAL INTERESTS / LEISURE ACTIVITIES

I'm cautious about including personal interests on a CV. Although some interviewers like to see it as it provides details on the whole person, it can also fuel their prejudices. Some people take a dislike to people with a certain hobby, for example. There is no way to know what the reader's prejudice may be, so it's best to be cautious.

Sometimes, people will write down things to make them look good. If you include reading for example, be ready to discuss your favourite author or what you are reading at the moment. When listing interests, it can help to expand a little. For example, writing not just *"running"*, but *"training to complete a half marathon in the Spring"*.

If you have an unusual hobby you may want to include it as it could get you short-listed if a potential employer is intrigued and wants to know more. When I used to apply for jobs, interviewers would always ask me about my hobby of English Civil War re-enactment. On one occasion, this led on to a discussion of how the war could have been avoided, and I was glad I could speak with some authority on the subject.

Organisational memberships

You may have gained skills and competence through membership of an organisation. If these skills are relevant to an employer, include them. Do you take part in environmental projects? Are you involved in a community action group, etc? If it could be relevant, then make a note.

Memberships might reveal some personal information (e.g., you are gay, a member of a particular religious or political group, etc.) but most people will not use this against you. (If they do, would you really want to work for them?)

STEP 4: CREATION PHASE

There are several styles of CV, but for now, let's take your initial work and create effectively written text. You can play around with the layout later.

It is important to be in a positive frame of mind when you produce your CV. No matter what your situation, you need to look for the high points of what you have achieved, not get side-tracked into worry over, for example, how long it may take you to get another job.

The whole point of the CV is to get you an interview, so put yourself in the position of the interviewer. For whatever job you are applying for, what are the most important things for the interviewer to know?

Section 1: The top of your CV will contain your personal details

All personal details except name, address and phone numbers should be at the end of your CV. Do include your email address, particularly if you are 'more mature', as it shows you are competent with new technology. Females need to think about whether to include Ms, Miss, or Mrs. I prefer to use my name without a title.

Make sure there is a professional answer-phone message on each phone number you provide. Just use your mobile number if there is a chance a family member could answer the phone in a less than professional way. Never include your work number.

Section 2: Profile or career summary

The Profile can be seen as an optional element of the CV. It gives the reader a concise overview of your skills, experience and aptitudes. As with all CVs, you will customize it for every job you apply for.

The biggest mistake people make is to focus on themselves and their needs. Think about it from the employers' point of view. They want someone to solve problems, so think about what it is that you can do for them, not the other way around. If you say:

> *"Seeking a position where I can utilize my skills and with potential for career advancement."*

This may sound fine to the person writing the CV, but it isn't focused on what the employer wants or needs. They will more than likely tell themselves, *"So what, that's what you want, but I want someone who can use their skills to solve my current problems."* So make sure you focus on the job, its requirements, and what you have to offer. Anything superfluous should be removed.

This was used by one of my clients and it resulted in an interview:

> *"Award-winning, highly accomplished Operations Manager with successful track records of consistently increasing revenue and slashing operating costs now seeking a new challenge where my skills and track record can be utilised in the facilities sector."*

KEY SKILLS

As most CVs are machine-read, include a list of the key skills needed for success in the particular job you are applying for; include them throughout your CV.

Section 3: Work History

This section, and the following one on education, may be interchangeable to suit individual circumstances. For example, if you are a recent graduate with a thin employment record, put *Education and Training* before *Work History.*

It is customary to set out your details in reverse chronological order covering the last 10-15 years of employment. Unless you are considering a complete career change, emphasis should be placed on your current or last position. That is what the reader will be particularly interested in. If you had a large number of jobs earlier in your career, or if your career goes back over many years, summarise this information as an 'earlier career' paragraph.

Include the minimum detail on your previous companies, as the CV is about **you**, not what the previous company did! However, one line with a succinct description of the company might be helpful.

If you have had a lot of jobs, put the dates on the right hand side. We read left to right, so the dates in this case, come across as less important.

Should your existing or past job titles be peculiar to your company or industry, express them in terms that are recognisable to the outside world.

If you have worked as a temp, your employer is the temping agency, not the company where you worked. Don't be tempted to state otherwise, as it could be seen as a reason for dismissal.

As you look at your jobs, have a look at the job title. Some companies give people fantastic job titles (look at all the Vice Presidents in American companies). So, if the job titles seem 'high', review what you write down. In some companies, everyone is a manager because they manage themselves, whereas in the Civil Service, the term 'officer' as part of a job title can refer to a quite senior role.

Sally worked as an HR Manager, and her next job was HR Director. (This was with a much smaller company, and she was not a director in the true sense; the work was less involved than in her previous job and she left after a year due to frustration and boredom). She then joined the council as Personnel Officer, and was now earning more than in the previous jobs but the job titles made this look like a *backward* step. She amended her CV to show HR Manager, HR Director and Government Personnel Officer, which ensured that the latter job was not seen by a recruiter as one with lower status.

The Work History section should emphasise and quantify key achievements. Think back to your daily duties. What good things were achieved because of what you did? Write them down, and the more specific the better. Using a bullet format makes it easier for the reader to notice the key points.

For example, instead of writing:

> *"Responsibilities included implementation of policies and procedures, training new employees, interfacing with subordinates and associates"*

…which is a bit of a mouthful, it's much more effective to say:

> *"I worked with staff and associates to increase product turnover by 15 percent and sales by 23 percent. Also trained 14 new employees, five of whom were rapidly promoted."*

You may want to add more to the achievements you listed earlier. For each achievement:

- What was the problem, situation or opportunity?

- What core skills, strengths or technical expertise did you use?

- What was the benefit of the action you took?

- Can you quantify any of these benefits in terms of money saved, time saved, reduction in staffing costs, etc?

As you review your job history, you may notice that several appointments have been held at similar levels in a relatively short space of time. It is important not to be perceived as a 'job hopper.' The problem can be overcome by incorporating several positions into one paragraph, for example:

1995-99 Quantity Surveyor

During this period, key positions were held with several multinational companies on fixed-term contracts including major development projects for Amec, Wimpey, Balfour Beatty etc.

Follow that with a summary of responsibilities and achievements throughout the period.

ACHIEVEMENT STATEMENTS

Too often, people fill their CV with descriptions of the tasks they do. But employers don't want to know the detail of your job description, rather what you have achieved and how you have stood out from the majority. As you put your bullet points under each job, avoid starting a statement with a qualification such as *"part of..."* If you write, *"My role involves dealing with customer enquiries, responding to orders and helping to produce end of month reports,"* a recruiter may think, *"So what, if that's how you spend your time; what did you actually achieve?"*

Here are some poor examples of what to include under career history. Paul had been advised to include the sorts of phrases and words that people would be looking for, but what do they mean?

- *"Allowing prospective employers to make use of my exemplary interpersonal and communication skills and diverse working environment experience."*

- *"Providing employers with the assurance of my intuitive, interpersonal and self management skills and the development of my business acumen."*

Make your achievements specific. Instead of "*duties included the supervision of staff*," replace that with "*successfully supervised and led a team of eight.*" Instead of "*responsible for departmental budget*" replace with "*personally controlled a budget in excess of £xxx.*" Instead of "*excellent verbal skills*," replace with, "*trained 24 new employees in customer service procedures.*"

Now review the achievements you listed in **step 1 of the preparation phase.** As a prompt, you might like to try to think of examples where you:

- Achieved a major objective.

- Contributed to a major decision.

- Handled an emergency situation.

- Reduced overheads, came in under budget.

- Saved time, money, equipment, facilities.

- Improved a product, services, or procedure.

- Consistently met deadlines.

- Received an award, special commendation or letter of thanks.

- Achieved sporting or social recognition.

- Improved team morale.

EXAMPLES OF ACHIEVEMENT STATEMENTS

You have now identified a number of statements – excellent! Now it's time to tighten the language and compare them to your various appointments. Before you do this, have a look at the following examples to give you some ideas. Note that wherever possible, there is a numerical result, improvement or outcome of some type. When referring to money, use 'k' to express thousands, e.g., £25k not 25,000 or 25 thousand. Use 'M' to express millions, e.g., £10M. You can also tighten words by, for example, replacing "*more than*" with "+." For example, change "*managed more than 50 staff*" to "*managed 50+ staff*".

- **Developed** a more integrated working relationship with the American parent company leading to significant economies of scale.

- **Introduced** a computerised Credit Control and Debt Collection system. This reduced debtor days from 55 to 44 within 6 months from introduction.

- **Cut inventory levels** by £1m over two years by introducing new inventory control procedures, at the same time improving stock availability by 10%.

- Successfully **set up** and ran a community centre for three years.

- Ensured IS09001 quality standards were met or **exceeded** and conducted regular quality audits leading to enhanced efficiencies which saved the company £0.5m.

- **Learned** new graphics package and used this to improve presentations for sales force. This was well received by clients and contributed to the company achieving a 20% increase in sales in my area.

- Devised and implemented a new sales training programme which resulted in a 37% increase in new business.

- Relocated business, systems and administration functions from London to Leeds, **saving** £4.6m over two years.

- **Introduced** a photocopy logging procedure, which was adopted throughout the company, saving £750 per month. Together with the Marketing Manager, designed and produced the company's quarterly catalogue.

- Fostered good relationships with new suppliers.

- Negotiated and improved terms and quality of supply, which reduced manufacturing costs by 60%.

- **Developed** a new system for generating sales leads which was adopted throughout the group, resulting in a 30% improvement in sales performance with the same number of sales executives.

- **Project-managed** each individual business system and personally designed, developed and implemented the financial accounting, grain trading and seed systems.

- On the strength of reputation as a firm yet caring leader, put in charge of low morale team of 30 medical and support personnel and **improved effectiveness** and discipline through developing good team spirit which helped motivate and bond the group.

- **Reduced** inventory by 25% within a year after installing a material control and forward-planning system.

POSITIVE ACTION WORDS

Each of your bullets should start with a positive action word. Use this list as a prompt for other words to use:

Accelerated, Accessed, Accomplished, Achieved, Acquainted, Acquired, Acted, Activated, Adapted, Added, Addressed, Adjusted, Administered, Advanced, Advertised, Advised, Aided, Allocated, Altered, Amended, Analysed, Answered, Anticipated, Applied, Appointed, Appraised, Approved, Arbitrated, Arranged, Ascertained, Asked, Assembled, Assessed, Assigned, Assisted, Attained, Attended, Audited, Augmented, Authored, Authorised, Automated, Averted, Awarded.

Balanced, Boosted, Briefed, Broadened, Brought, Budgeted, Built.

Calculated, Calmed, Canvassed, Captured, Catalogued, Categorised, Chaired, Challenged, Charted, Checked, Choreographed, Clarified, Classified, Coached, Collaborated, Collected, Combined, Comforted, Communicated, Compared, Competed, Compiled, Completed, Composed, Compounded, Computed, Conceived, Conceptualised, Condensed, Conducted, Conserved, Considered, Consolidated, Constructed, Consulted, Contacted, Contracted, Contributed, Controlled, Conveyed, Convinced, Corrected, Correlated, Corresponded, Counselled, Crafted, Created, Criticised, Critiqued, Cultivated, Customised, Cut.

Debated, Debugged, Decided, Decreased, Deduced, Defined, Defused, Delegated, Delighted, Delivered, Demonstrated, Depreciated,

Described, Designated, Designed, Detailed, Detected, Determined, Developed, Devised, Devoted, Diagnosed, Diagrammed, Directed, Disciplined, Disclosed, Discovered, Dispatched, Dispensed, Displayed, Disproved, Dissected, Disseminated, Dissuaded, Distributed, Diversified, Diverted, Documented, Doubled, Drafted, Dramatised, Drew, Drove.

Earned, Edited, Educated, Effected, Elaborated, Elected, Elevated, Elicited, Eliminated, Emphasised, Employed, Enabled, Encouraged, Endorsed, Enforced, Engineered, Enhanced, Enlisted, Enriched, Ensured, Established, Estimated, Evaluated, Examined, Exceeded, Excelled, Excited, Executed, Exhibited, Expanded, Expedited, Experimented, Exploited, Explored, Expressed, Extended, Extracted, Extrapolated.

Fabricated, Facilitated, Familiarised, Fashioned, Filed, Finalised, Financed, Fixed, Focused, Followed, Forecasted, Formalised, Formed, Formulated, Fostered, Found, Framed, Fulfilled.

Gained, Gathered, Generated, Governed, Grew, Guarded, Guided.

Handled, Harnessed, Hastened, Headed, Helped, Highlighted, Hired.

Identified, Illustrated, Imagined, Implemented, Improvised, Incorporated, Increased, Inferred, Influenced, Informed, Initiated, Innovated, Inspected, Inspired, Installed, Instated, Instigated, Instilled, Instituted, Instructed, Insured, Integrated, Interested, Interpreted, Interviewed, Introduced, Invented, Investigated, Issued.

Joined, Judged, Justified.

Kept.

Launched, Learnt, Lectured, Led, Leveraged, Licensed, Lifted, Lightened, Linked, Liquidated, Listened, Lobbied, Logged.

Made, Maintained, Managed, Manipulated, Marketed, Mastered, Maximised, Mediated, Memorised, Mentored, Merged, Met, Minimised, Mobilised, Modelled, Moderated, Modernised, Modified, Monitored, Motivated.

Named, Narrated, Navigated, Negotiated, Nurtured.

Observed, Obtained, Offset, Opened, Operated, Orchestrated, Ordered, Organised, Oriented, Originated, Oversaw.

Participated, Perceived, Performed, Persuaded, Pinpointed, Pioneered, Planed, Practiced, Praised, Predicted, Prepared, Prescribed, Presented, Preserved, Presided, Prevailed, Prevented, Prioritised, Probed, Processed, Procured, Produced, Programmed, Projected, Promoted, Proposed, Protected, Proved, Provided, Provoked, Publicised, Published, Purchased.

Quadrupled, Quantified, Questioned.

Raised, Read, Realised, Reasoned, Received, Recognised, Recommended, Reconciled, Recorded, Recruited, Redesigned, Reduced, Reengineered, Referred, Refined, Registered, Regulated, Rehabilitated, Related, Remembered, Remodelled, Rendered, Reorganised, Repaired, Replaced, Reported, Represented, Requested, Researched, Resolved, Responded, Restored, Restructured, Retrieved, Revamped, Reversed, Reviewed, Revised, Revitalised, Revolutionised, Rewarded, Routed.

Saved, Scheduled, Screened, Searched, Secured, Segmented, Selected, Sensed, Separated, Served, Serviced, Set, Settled, Sewed, Shaped, Shared, Shopped, Showed, Simplified, Sketched, Sold, Solicited, Solved, Sorted, Sparked, Specified, Spoke, Sponsor, Stabilised, Staffed, Staged, Started, Stimulated, Streamlined, Strengthened, Stretched, Structured, Studied, Submitted, Succeeded, Summarised, Sung, Superseded, Supervised, Supplemented, Supplied, Supported, Surpassed, Surveyed, Symbolised, Synthesised, Systemised.

Tailored, Talked, Targeted, Tended, Terminated, Tested, Thanked, Thought, Thrived, Told, Took, Traced, Tracked, Traded, Trained, Transacted, Transcribed, Transferred, Translated, Travelled, Treated, Trimmed, Tripled, Troubleshot, Turned, Tutored, Typed.

Umpired, Uncovered, Understood, Understudied, Unified, Unravelled, Updated, Upgraded, Used, Utilised.

Validated, Verbalised, Verified, Viewed, Volunteered.

Widened, Withdrew, Won, Write.

Section 4: Education and training

You have already collected details on your education and training courses, so now you will review this to choose what is most appropriate for each particular job you seek.

Don't overload this section with lists of dates, schools, university etc. Include only what's appropriate for the job. (As you get older, you don't need to include details of your earlier education.) Also include specialist training and professional qualifications. List the courses in order of significance. If you have attended a large number of courses, list only those that are relevant to the post that you are applying for to ensure that they are noted and considered.

Are you a member of any professional organisation? Perhaps you do not have full membership yet, but are an associate or affiliate. Include this information here.

Section 5: Interests

If there is space, you can include any interests that are relevant or might serve as a comfortable topic for discussion at interview. Think about which of your interests can be used to demonstrate qualities of leadership, fitness, intellectual capacity etc. Also include committee memberships, including those you have held in the past. When including interests, try to select those that fall into the following categories: active or sport, group or team, or creative. Make sure they are real interests you can describe if challenged.

Section 6: Optional personal details

It is in the last section that you can include other relevant information such as a full, clean driving license or willingness to relocate (if you are). Some people include details on marital status, children, nationality, etc. My personal view is not to include them unless you believe it will give you an 'edge' for a particular job vacancy.

Your Career Summary, version 2

Earlier you completed your first attempt. You can now review what you wrote and amend it to suit each job you apply for. Make sure you have focused on what you can offer and your enthusiasm for the job, rather than on what you can get from the job.

> Shorter is better. This should not spread to 1/3 of a page; just 2–3 lines make much more impact.

Read through these examples, to see what others have done.

- *An experienced, very adaptable Manufacturing Manager with professional training and a good understanding of Total Productive Maintenance. An able communicator at all levels who is both objective and pragmatic. Works well under pressure and remains calm in difficult situations. Used to working with little or no supervision and on own initiative.*

- *An experienced and innovative manager who has led a multi-skilled team through difficult and changing times with inspirational and influential leadership.*

- *Excellent people management and problem solving abilities, coupled with a strong desire to work in a 'get things right' environment and the aptitude to motivate others, are the strengths which have been called on most in the past three years.*

- *A responsible and mature business manager with substantial experience of retail and wholesale banking with a major UK Clearing Bank. Highly developed aptitude for customer liaison, most recently used as a Financial Consultant and previously as a Client Service Manager. Strong interpersonal communication skills, supported by a high degree of commitment and integrity. Fluent German.*

THE SKILLS-BASED CV

In a skills-based CV, the main focus is on the skills, activities and achievements that best represent your suitability for new employment, with no account of where the experience was gained. This is followed by a summary of your career history, and then education and training relevant to the position sought.

Skills-based headings

Provide highly focused paragraphs on specific skills and abilities as **this CV encourages the reader to initially focus on your abilities and skills.** This helps a recruiter to clearly see how you measure up to the requirements of the job.

With a skills-based CV, you list your experience under a number of headings chosen to be relevant to the job you are applying for. For example, administration, communications, consulting, counselling, design, engineering, human resources, management, planning, research, sales, training, and writing.

As you review the job you are applying for, pick out the key elements of it and provide examples under each heading. Put these headings in descending order of importance with up to a maximum of six headings.

Having created your headings, use 2–5 bullets with specific examples of what you have achieved relating to each heading. These examples can be drawn from both your work and personal life.

Brief employment history

An organisation will want to know who you have worked for, but as this is not the main focus, it comes after the skills-based headings. I would keep this brief but would include employer, job title and dates. Some people will decide to leave out this section, but doing so creates the impression you have something to hide and you may not get short listed.

Education/Qualifications/Training

As with any style of CV, include details on secondary schooling and university alongside qualifications, including relevant short courses you have attended.

Interests and positions of responsibility

Include them if they will enhance your application.

EXAMPLE CVS

Too many CVs are based on templates and look like it. You can see from Kim's initial CV that there is a lot of room for improvement:

- The tiny print for contact details.

- The lack of dates for education and training.

- Professional skills mixing up catering and business skills. (Unless she wants to work in catering, this detracts from the relevant qualification.)

- The way a number of jobs are listed within just two job titles.

- The lack of her achievements.

13b Mill Lane
Macclesfield
Cheshire
SK11 5TG

Phone 07931 567xxx
E-mail kim.x@yahoo.co.uk

Kim Richardson

Profile   I am a reliable and hardworking property lawyer with the ability to work on my own initiative. I work with enthusiasm and enjoy a challenge. I am committed and flexible with good interpersonal and communication skills. I can deal professionally with a diverse range of people and motivate colleagues. I prioritise my workload and work effectively under pressure

Education/Training

Loretto Convent 1979 – O'Levels Achieved

English Language, English Literature, Human Biology, Food and Nutrition, French and Religious Studies

St Peters School 1981 – A' Levels Achieved

English and Food and Nutrition

Manchester Polytechnic 1981- 1984

HND in Hotel Catering and Institutional Management

South Manchester college and distance learning from the Institute of Legal Executives. 2001 - 2006

Level 3 passed

Level 4 passed Probate and Succession, Land Law, Conveyancing Practice and Landlord and Tenant

Qualified as a Fellow of the Institute in June 2008

Professional Skills

Salon Culinaire silver award

Proficient in use of computer software accountancy packages

Royal Institute of Public Health and Hygiene Certificate with Merit

Hotel and Catering Industry Training Board certificates in Organisational

Training and Assessment. Group Training Techniques and Trainer Skills 1

Proficient in use of DPS and Eclipse legal case management systems

Member of the local branch of the Institute of Legal Executives

Director of Winston Management Ltd the company managing the freehold of the flats where I live

European Computer Driving Licence (ECDL) commenced course and studying Modules 1 and 2

Employment Experience

2002 – 2008 Wilson and Foster Solicitors. Stockport

Legal Executive

Conveyancing work from instruction to completion consisting of sales and purchases for both freehold and leasehold properties.

Equity Release, remortgages and transfers of equity.

Preparing contract reports. financial completion statements and arranging client meetings in the office.

Achieved and exceeded fee targets

I deputised in Solicitors and Partners absence

Plan and implement marketing strategies for the firm

Represent the firm at corporate and client entertaining events

Excellent client survey responses received post completion

Effectively communicating with estate agents, mortgage brokers, surveyors and other Solicitors

1988 – 2002 Gardner Merchant Management Services North West Division

District Support Manager

Responsible for the implementation and review of company control systems

Ensure that financial targets exceeded and costs controlled

Responsible for training and developing Catering Managers

Team manager

Liasing with clients and senior executives of the company.

Successfully marketing additional services to increase profits and ensure contract retention

Deputising for the District Manager in the highest earning area of the business

References

Supplied on request

Now look at Kim's revised CV and see the difference!

- Contact details are much clearer.
- Employment includes specific examples of what she has achieved in two different roles.
- The catering experience is divided into three different jobs.
- The education includes dates, and the business elements of the hotel and catering HND are highlighted.
- Professional skills are divided between hotel and catering and business.

Kim Richardson

13b Mill Lane, Macclesfield, Cheshire SK11 5TG
H 01625 277XXX M 07931 567 xxx
E-mail: kimXX@yahoo.co.uk

A Legal Executive with experience of acting for high profile clients in a professional manner. Kim works with enthusiasm, enjoys a challenge and prioritises work effectively under pressure. Excellent communication skills together with a high level of commitment and integrity resulting in excellent client care survey comments. Confident at problem solving, with attention to detail and good organisational skills, Kim has successfully completed complicated transactions working on own initiative.

Career History

Legal Executive, Wilson and Foster Solicitors

July 2004 – July 2008

- Residential conveyancer working on a varied caseload consisting of freehold and leasehold sales and purchases including new builds, equity release, remortgages and transfers of equity including both probate and matrimonial matters.
- Exceeded fee target by £30,000 in first year working as a fee earner.
- Deputised in Solicitors and partners absence across all 3 branches, demonstrating flexibility.
- Saved the firm money on expensive locum costs by assisting locums who were only employed part-time.
- Planned and implemented marketing strategies for the firm, successfully establishing good relationships with local Estate Agents to increase number of referrals and improve level of fees.
- Achieved objective of completing the Legal Executive course, passing all exams required to qualify as a Fellow whilst working full time.
- Responsible for the people management of two secretaries, working well as a team even during exceptionally busy periods.
- Providing a high level of Customer Service with excellent post completion client survey responses together with many letters of thanks.

Paralegal, Wilson and Foster Solicitors

January 2002 – July 2004

- Assisted three fee earners consisting of two Legal Executives and one Partner with the administration and correspondence on all their files.
- Responsible for completing contracts, deeds, transfers and property information forms.
- Carried out research both on line and in the firm's library to obtain copies of Acts of Parliament and case notes.
- Resolved outstanding issues to close backlog of files ready for archiving, resulting in additional revenue to the company through finalising unpaid invoices.

Support Manager, Gardner Merchant Management Services, Southern Division

January 1996 – January 2002

Responsible for training and developing a team of 15 Catering Managers In the following areas:

- **Budgets** – planning and ensuring financial targets were exceeded and costs controlled.
- **Food hygiene and safety standards** – monitoring practice to ensure compliance with company and legislative requirements.
- **Recruitment** – assisting with the interview and selection process for various roles
- Management of large, complex catering events such as Gourmet dinners.
- Achieved a bonus of £250 for improving standards at a new site and ensuring staff were both motivated and enthusiastic.

- Actively increasing revenue by providing sales leads which were successfully converted into contracts for both cleaning and vending services and receiving a selection of gifts as a reward.
- Deputised for the District Manager where appropriate in the highest earning area of the business sector and receiving a letter of thanks from the Operations Director.
- Carried out audits throughout the District on all Personnel and Training records and successfully achieving the Investors in People Award for the division.
- Project managed and co-ordinate the opening of a prestigious contract at large multiple sites.

Assistant Manager, Gardner Merchant, Barclays Bank (Radbrook Hall)
August 1992 – January 1996

Responsible for the smooth and efficient transfer of the Catering Operations from in-house to Gardner Merchant at a time when existing staff resisted change. Implementing all the company procedures

- Deputising for the manager during periods of absence.
- Training, developing and managing a team of 25.
- Organised special functions for VIPs and received a handwritten thank you letter from the Chief Accountant for Barclays.

Area Relief Manager, Gardner Merchant, North West Division
September 1988 – August 1992

- Provided both chef and management cover for all Catering Managers during periods of
- absence.
- Assisted the Area Support Manager and Area Manager with the opening of new contracts
- during a period of rapid growth.
- During hurricanes in 1990 provide emergency cover at the weekend providing hot meals for
- Electricians at short notice

Education & Professional Qualifications

1973 – 1979	Loretto Convent 6 O'Levels, grades B – C including English
1979 – 1981	St Peters School A'Levels in English D and Home Economics C
1981 – 1984	**Manchester Polytechnic - HND in Hotel Catering and Institutional Management** Covered: Business Administration I (Accounts), Management and Business Administration II, Marketing Accommodation and House Services, Food and Beverage Management
2001 – 2006	**South Manchester College and distance learning - Legal Executive Course from the Institute of Legal Executives,** Passed Levels 3 and 4 in Probate and Succession, Land Law, Conveyancing Practice and Landlord.
2008	**Qualified as a Fellow of the Institute**
2008	Learn Direct **City and Guilds in Maths, Pass**

Professional Skills

Hotel and Catering Training Board Certificate in Trainer Skills 1, 1985
Hotel and Catering Training Board Certificate in Organising Training and Assessment and Craft Trainer Award, 1992
Royal Institute of Public Health and Hygiene Certificate in Food Hygiene with Credit, 1996
Proficient in DPS and Eclipse legal case management systems, 2002 - 2008
European Computer Driving Licence (ECDL) commenced course and passed Module 2, 2008

Travel – I have recently returned from a round the world trip stopping in Los Angeles, Fiji, Sydney and Hong Kong.

Full clean driving licence

and here's a skills-based CV:

Vicky Hudson

62 Benson Street, Northwich, Cheshire CW9 5XX
T: 01606 556 XXX M: 07931 344 XXX
E: vhudson@gmail.com

"Simply outstanding administration skills"
"You can rely on Vicky to get a job done and with a high attention to detail"

Key areas of expertise

High level team administration

- Taking minutes of team meetings using excellent shorthand
- Taking notes at grievance meetings, e.g. pay disputes, and staff stepping "out of line", maintaining confidentiality
- Coordinating and minuting the Northwich Tackling Drug and Alcohol Together Group
- Preparing duty manager rotas

Computer Skills

- **Word:** including mail merge, tracking changes, creating forms and templates Completed advanced course (2003)
- **Sage HR:** database for personnel – created reports for sickness and holidays for Different teams
- **Power Point:** creating presentations
- **Excel:** can produce spreadsheets and formulas

General administration

- Ordering stationary, photocopying, monitoring petty cash, faxing, scanning and Dealing with mail
- Facilities management – arranging for repairs to be undertaken, new carpets fitted etc.

Support to the company secretary and chief executive

- Various tasks including preparing and circulating board papers
- Sensitive note taking at senior management business meetings

HR Administration – Recruitment *Extensive experience*

- **Preparation:** drafting the ad, liaison with agency, producing information packs, Collecting names and distribution, receiving application and collating ready for short listing
- **Interview:** sending out letters, preparing paper work and excercises, arranging Schedules, looking after candidates
- **Post Interview:** Sending out letter to successful and unsuccessful, requesting references, creating and setting out contracts

HR Administration – Payroll and sickness monitoring

- Collating information on a monthly basis related to annual leave
- Preparing monthly spreadsheets related to sickness monitoring

Training administration (*Working with the Work Force Development Manager*)

- Administrator for core training for all staff – sourced a venue and trainer, set up venue, informed staff of date, collected names and allocated to courses. Collated evaluation forms onto spread sheets.

Legal Secretary

- Typing letters, legal documents and statements, general admin duties
- Experienced in probate, conveyancing and litigation, attending court and taking notes
- Producing detailed bills; contact with clients – in person or by telephone

Employment

xxxx Trust – Drug Addictions Agency   **1996-2008**
Counsel people with drug addiction – 4 offices with 15 staff across the North West
HR Administrator :   **2006-2008**
Senior Administrator :   **2004-2006**
Administrator :   **1996-2006**
Supporting the community alcohol team and volunteers
- Reception duties, sourcing rehabs, mentoring volunteers, producing display stands
- Mentoring volunteer staff to obtain NVQ qualifications
- Office management including managing a tenant company
- Running reception for weekly specialist clinics for consultant and CPN
- Inputting and updating database of service users, using a tailor made package
- Covering admin in other offices – Warrington, Widnes, Crewe

Word Processing Operative, Technical Services Department, Vale Royal Council
April – December 1995 (Maternity cover)
The technical services department covered planning permissions, estimates for resurfacing, trees etc.

Secretary, Treemont Consultants   1993-
1995
Recruitment agency where I supported the 4 partners
Typing and administration, produced mail shots, sourced suitable candidates.

Legal Secretary,   **1970 – 1983**
Secretary, Hayes and Simpson: 1970-1972
Secretary to partner, Robinson-Chase: 1972 - 1980
Secretary to litigation partner, Judith Morrison: 1981-1983

Education

Relevant education includes:

RSA: Typing Levels 1, 2 and 3, Shorthand to 80 wpm, Secretarial duties, Audio-typing,
English Language – Level 1 and 2; Pitman: Shorthand to 90 wpm
NVQ D32/33 – Business admin (1988)
London Chamber of Commerce – French to intermediate level (1993/94)
CLAIT Level 1 (1994)
RSA : Word Processing (1989-1991)
GCE 'O' Level – English and Commerce (1970)

A variety of short courses including : Diversity, Equal opportunities, Customer care, Dealing
with difficult situations, Master class – Absence monitoring conference in London, Master class
seminar in HR admin in London, Display techniques, Minute taking course, advanced
Training in Word and Excel

Full clean driving license

Photographs

Some people include a photograph as part of their CV, within the layout. I've discussed this with fellow recruiters and we agree that if a photograph is needed, it should be sent separately and should only be included when personal image is an important job element. Then it must be of high quality and not a holiday snap.

THE TEXT-BASED CV

Most internet job sites and on line application forms will want you to paste your CV into boxes. Starting with a plain text version means you won't get unusual symbols as their software strips out your formatting.

How to create a text-based CV

Don't play about with your Word document, instead save it as a text file or copy it into a text editing programme such as Notepad. Once you open it, you will see you have lost all formatting such as underlines, bold, fonts, etc.

You can improve the layout by using a hard return (use the big 'Enter' button to start a new line). It might look OK in a word processing programme, but it can be very difficult to read via a text package without hard returns. Try it out if you want to see for yourself. You can make improvements to the style if you use CAPITAL LETTERS as headers.

Make sure you include all contact details on their own line, with a hard return in between.

KEY WORDS

When a CV is uploaded to a jobs database, companies will search for relevant candidates using key words. So you want to choose **as many key words as possible** to increase your opportunity to match your suitability for jobs and to increase the number of 'hits' you can attract. You can **identify words by reviewing advertisements for similar vacancies** and using them in your CV. For example, for an IT job, include Java, relational databases, etc. For a job in accounting, use financial statement, inventory, etc.

Use enough key words to define your skills, experience, education, professional affiliations, etc. Increase your list of key words by including specifics. For example, list the names of software programmes you use such as Microsoft Word. You can enhance your chance of success by linking each key word with a specific achievement which expands on that key word, e.g., how you have been using the software, for how long, and on what projects.

When searching for specific experience, the **company will search by entering key words (usually nouns)** such as writer, MBA, marketing manager, engineer, Japanese (in the case of language fluency), London, etc. So the more attention you pay to choosing the right key words, the better.

STYLE AND LAYOUT

Review your CV against the following:

Is it focused? Make sure it sounds positive, strong, and to the point. Be concise, and clear, and make sure every word helps make the pitch. For example, if you are an academic, use an addendum for research papers. If your CV covers a page and a half, do not be tempted to fill the space.

Does it grab attention? Will it grab the reader's attention in the first 10 seconds? Avoid lengthy lists of responsibilities and job functions, because they just become boring. Highlight only achievements that will benefit the employer. Describe how your work has led to measurable outcomes benefiting your organisation.

Is it easy to follow? Keep to a logical pattern following conventions. With a chronological CV, always start with the most recent job and work backwards. To ensure there are no gaps in dates, use only years since leaving school, or be prepared to explain the gap. If you were self-employed or at home to bring up a family, say so! Explain your current role. Do not assume people will know what your responsibilities are. Use present tense verbs for your current job, and past tense verbs for all previous jobs.

Is it well laid out? Does it include a clear summary or objective? Is this focused on the needs of the company rather than on your wants? Have you used action statements and not vague terms? Rather than using the general comment *"excellent communication skills"*, it would be more effective to put *"Wrote jargon-free user guide for 10,000 readers."*

Are all the words used in their simplest form? You don't want to make the person doing the short-listing feel inferior if they don't understand your superabundance of polysyllabic terminology (your use of too many big words!). As another example, don't *"interface"* with people; *"work"* with them.

Review the layout - Margins should be at least one inch wide. Don't make smaller margins so you can fit in more words. Less is more, and decent sized margins will help your CV to stand out. For layout, use the tab key to make sure columns line up. To fit more on a page, you can use an 8pt font for the space lines or change the heading. You can also reduce the character spacing on the font by 0.2 points. If you do this, do it throughout the document. What font will you use? Times New Roman is easy to read; Arial, Tahoma and Verdana are all popular. Use bold formatting for your name and section headings and to emphasise key words. Use *italics* for the names of publications and foreign phrases, if any. Use just two font sizes, and avoid ALL CAPS and too much underlining. Do not justify the text. A ragged right edge is much easier to read. Put your name in the footer using a smaller type-face. Put the dates on the right hand side if you want to de-emphasise them.

Read and read again - You must re-read your CV: once for accuracy (numbers, city names, etc.), once for missing/extra words, and once more for spelling. Use a dictionary to be certain. Then, show your CV to several friends and ask them to read it out loud. Listen to where they put the emphasis as it might reveal that you've written something that's confusing or inaccurate. After you get their feedback, read through your CV once more and make any changes until it's 100% error-free. Don't rely too heavily on your spell-checker, because it will not catch misused yet properly spelled words like sun or son, site or sight, etc. And when you do use it, make sure it's set to UK or US English as appropriate.

Check that your CV is free of jargon. We often use abbreviations and anachronisms in our everyday language (TQM, BPI), or internal descriptions for job roles which have little meaning for others. Also make sure everything is easy to follow and ask the people who read your CV if they understand it.

If posting, don't staple pages. When the staple is removed for copying, the pages may tear. If using high quality paper, you could use both sides. It is not necessary to bind your CV or place it in a folder.

FINALISING YOUR CV

You are now reaching the completion of your CV. Please check against the following. If you cannot answer yes to every question, go back and make revisions until you can.

	YES	NO
Is it achievement-orientated? (as opposed to a list of what the job involved)	☐	☐
Are the verbs in the 'active' tense?	☐	☐
Is it structured in your favour? (Do you really want to tell them you are an unqualified sixty-year-old before they read of your chief executive experience?)	☐	☐
Does it emphasise your special skills?	☐	☐
Does it emphasise special achievements outside work?	☐	☐
Have you avoided any 'gaps' which would cause interviewer anxieties?	☐	☐
Is what you have done quantified where appropriate? (Interviewers love the use of numbers – how much money did you save? What time did you save?)	☐	☐
Have you used significant or emphasising adjectives? (Excellent experience, sole responsibility.)	☐	☐
Do the 'page breaks' make the reader want to turn the page?	☐	☐
Are you saying what you can do for the employer? Focusing on benefits?	☐	☐
Are you telling them only what they need to know?	☐	☐

Your CV is ready for sending. If you email it, ask for a receipt so you know it has arrived. If you post it:

- Print using a high quality print setting and on good quality paper (not photocopy quality but 100gsm).

- Choose a pale colour, ideally either bright white or cream. Pastel blue or pale grey are also options. **Using cream will make sure it stands out from the rest.** Your CV may be photocopied, and dark coloured paper doesn't photocopy well.

- Place your CV **unstapled** in a good quality envelope.

- Either write neatly or type on the envelope. If you claim computer expertise, use your computer to address the envelope, thus making your software-savvy claims more credible.

Do I really need more than one CV?

If you are clear on the type of job you are looking for, you will need only one CV. However, if you are looking for different types of jobs you will need a CV to address each type. For example, earlier in my career, my background made me suitable for the roles of counsellor, trainer, project manager or psychologist. Therefore, I would have emphasised different achievements depending on the job I was looking for.

CV DISTRIBUTION SERVICES

I am sometimes asked if a client should use a CV distribution service. My answer is always no!

First of all, you don't know who will receive it, and it may be sent for a job you would prefer not to apply for; or in some cases, you might have preferred to send a more customised application.

If you apply via an agency, it will cost the employer a lot more to employ you than if you had contacted them directly. For this reason, companies would rather deal with you directly.

Finally, what happens when you have finished your job search? How do you get the CVs removed and destroyed?

AND FINALLY...

You should now have a CV that will get results and is ready to use when applying to job ads and when networking. If you still lack confidence in your CV or need additional support or guidance, do as much as you can then contact a job search specialist such as Denise to arrange a personal review.

The key points I want you to remember from this chapter are:

- Review your CV for each application. It may just need a tweak, it may be fine, or you may need to include more elements that are relevant to the job.

- You may need to use your CV again, either for promotion or due to company changes. Review and update it on a regular basis.

Chapter Six

LINKEDIN

You have to be on LinkedIn. It's vital for online networking and essential to be in with a chance of being found by recruiters, but you must be fully involved. Too many people have a partly completed profile without even a photo. It gives a very poor impression and no wonder people think LinkedIn isn't worth pursuing. You wouldn't send a half finished CV when you apply for a job. To get 100% complete you need to also have at least 3 recommendations, so make sure you get an 'almost completed profile' before you start approaching people.

LinkedIn is the leading social networking site for professionals. Worldwide over 65 million professionals use LinkedIn to exchange information, ideas and opportunities. Over 3m users are based in the UK. You have the possibility to connect with people in your desired industry and an option to join relevant groups - there are more than 500,000 to choose from.

HOW LINKEDIN IS USED BY RECRUITERS

When recruiters use LinkedIn they start with an advanced search feature for people, scan the summaries of the profiles, any that are incomplete will be discarded. They will notice if you have a picture and if it is professional. They will then read recommendations and review the CV if one is uploaded. If they don't find any viable candidates they will search again, which could also include searching for people who are working/have worked for a specific company.

SAB Miller used LinkedIn to find 120 managers around the world, saving £1.2m in fees. In March 2010, Accenture publicised that they were going to hire 50,000 people and planned to recruit at least 40% of them via social media.

Using LinkedIn for research

Most people on LinkedIn already have jobs and so are happy to share with and help others, such as in researching companies and clients before a sales call, and seeking advice from people in a similar role but a different company. You can ask questions on a whole range of topics pertaining to the trends in a particular industry, or whether a particular MBA programme is right for you etc.

LET'S GET YOU STARTED

Set up an account at www.linkedin.com and add all relevant details. Early in the process it suggests you connect to your Yahoo/Gmail/Hotmail and such accounts to start connecting with people. I suggest you skip this step, you can do this later when you have completed as much of your profile as possible. You then need to confirm your email address, and your account is set up. You can review and edit anything you have already included.

Further details to add include location; this is useful as a recruiter could be searching for people within, for example, a 50-mile radius of Portsmouth.

You have 120 characters to create a professional headline, so make good use of them – I've used 114 characters.

Denise Taylor (previously Zaremba) (you)
Award Winning Career Coach and Author of "How to Get a Job in a Recession" - career coaching and career management
Gloucester, United Kingdom   Professional Training & Coaching

Use a job title that will be easily recognisable, not something that is very specific to your particular company; you want it to be a title that will grab the attention of a recruiter. So, 'Management Accountant' is quite bland, and you need to choose something that is more eye catching. You could list the position that you are seeking, either by being very specific or more general – 'Denise is seeking a position as an IT project manager'.

This professional headline will be included each time you appear on LinkedIn – whether it be for a status update or to ask or answer a question – so you want it to stand out.

A photo is essential and makes you more approachable. It's the first thing people will see as they open your LinkedIn profile. If you don't think you take a great photo it will be worth paying to have a professional one taken. **Do not even think of contacting people without your photo included, it significantly reduces the chance that people will accept your connection.**

Your summary and specialities are your chance to sell yourself. Think about the words that a recruiter might be searching for, and make sure to include them. You probably already have key words in your CV so include them here as well. You must include the words a recruiter would search for.

You could just copy in material from your CV but think about what is going to show you as more marketable. **You want the content to be compelling.**

Additional information

You can link 3 web pages to your profile. They can include those of the company you are working for, your blog or website, or an article you have had published online. Most people use 'My Blog' or 'My Website' but you can change these to include the actual name of your blog or to use a keyword such as in **'Personal feature on myself in The Lawyer'** or **'Denise Taylor's personal website'**. If you have a Twitter account you can include a link to your twitter page.

Claim your name! The default URL is a less than memorable mix of numbers and letters. Make it easier to be found by including your name. Mine is ***http://uk.linkedin.com/in/denisetaylor***. If you have a common name you may need to include your middle initial or name. A client added MBA to his name and he now appears first via a search for people with quite a common name.

Choose your privacy settings. You do this via the 'Account & Settings' tab at the top of your profile. Make sure that your 'public profile' is set to display full profile information so that it's accessible to search engines.

Getting ready to connect

Wait until your profile is complete, including previous employers names. It is unlikely that people will accept your connection if your profile is only partly done.

Use key words and phrases relevant to your target and niche. Make sure the type of work you seek is included in your professional headline and summary, and a couple of times in your professional section. But make sure it flows – it has to be an interesting read.

100% complete

You need 3 recommendations before your profile is 100% complete. But you can get everything else done first. Make sure that you have as many of the following completed as possible:

- A current position
- 2 past positions
- Education details
- Profile summary
- Profile photo
- Specialities

If you are a recent graduate without a work history, you can now include optional sections detailing group projects, honours and awards, involvement in organisations, test scores and courses.

Status update box

This allows you to provide updates on specifics that you are working on, for example: an event you are presenting at or attending, a significant accomplishment at work, a blog post or article you have published. Aim to update this several times a week.

Seeking connections

Upload your address book. You can then start to contact people. **Do not use the default message to everyone**; take the time to personalise it and, ideally, to personalise it with a short message perhaps including how you know somebody. Look to companies you have worked with and ask to connect with people who will know you. You can later seek recommendations from them. Also look up friends from school and university; you may be surprised by what they are now doing.

Do not just send out the standard message; use a personal message that demonstrates some thought.

Look at all the business cards you have collected; can you think of a reason to connect with the people who gave you them? Once you have connected with the people you already know, you can seek to connect with 'second level contacts', the people whom your contacts know.

LinkedIn LIONS

If you want more connections, go to *www.toplinked.com* and link to those with the largest number of connections. This will connect you with LinkedIn LIONS – these are 'open networkers' who will accept your invitation to connect so you can grow your contact list dramatically overnight.

Seeking groups

There are over 500,000 groups on LinkedIn! You can search for LinkedIn groups that relate to your company, industry, school or career interests. You can join a maximum of 50 groups and this is a great way to make contacts and develop relationships. Find 10 groups as a first step, and become active, not passive. You can choose between

- Industry-specific groups
- Trade and professional groups
- Employer alumni groups
- University groups
- Career-related groups
- Functional groups
- Personal interest groups

Each group will operate slightly differently; some may automatically grant you access, but at other times your application will be reviewed. Review any particular guidelines before you post. Each group includes links to discussions, news, jobs and sometimes subgroups.

Look to ask questions but also answer questions and respond to posts. This will raise your visibility. I suggest you join at least 3 LinkedIn groups that are specific to your industry and participate in discussions on a daily basis, both posting questions and replying to others.

Recommendations

People pay attention to recommendations, and you should seek out these from people you have worked with in the past. You could suggest to them the sort of job you are looking for and your key attributes, skills and achievements so they can write with this in mind. Recommendations don't have to be long, and you may find that past bosses and colleagues are happy to write this brief reference for you. You can remind them of what you have done. Also recommend others – be specific in what you say.

If you are being made redundant ask your manager for a recommendation before you leave. The recommendation will let other people know that you were valued. As the manager you can also ask for a recommendation, possibly focused on your leadership qualities.

Researching

LinkedIn is brilliant for helping with your job search. You can use it to research companies and to identify job opportunities. Alongside using Google to research companies, you can find out much more via LinkedIn – names of people who work there, or details on their background and education.

You may feel uncomfortable in contacting someone who currently works for the company and who you barely know, so another option is to contact people who used to work for the company; they are more likely to be willing to talk freely about the company. Do think about what you can do in return.

As you research companies that interest you, review individual profiles. You may see that people in the jobs you aspire to all belong to a specific professional association; if so, go ahead and join, aim to attend some meetings.

Think about the companies you want to work for and see if there's anyone you know who works for these companies. You can then contact them and ask for referrals.

Look up the people who work for the company that interests you; look at the companies they have previously worked for, and also the companies where they move to – it could provide interesting career paths to review.

HOW TO NETWORK ON LINKEDIN

To develop your network you can get involved in discussions, answer questions, post articles and contribute content.

Introductions

You can ask to be connected to someone who is connected to a member of your network. It can help your contact if you create a short email that they can then send on to the person you want to connect with. Write it as if it is from them, so that the changes they need to make are minimal. Draw out your achievements and include details to compel somebody to connect to you.

I worked with Andrew who was keen to extend his connections to help him move into a new career path of Organisational Development. He joined a number of networks and identified a number of people to contact. I worked with him to develop a clear way of making contact, demonstrating some connection and making sure the message was highly personalised. This was not an easy task; it took time and he had to wait for people to get back to him. Andrew expected everyone to say 'yes' and provide help; I reassured him that getting 4 out of 10 to respond was a great move.

For other people, he needed to make contact via someone else, but even with a personalised welcome message not everyone agreed. Of those who did connect, some proved extremely helpful and more were useful. Andrew made sure to get back in touch to say thank you, and I've encouraged him to stay in touch.

Just because somebody has someone as a connection it doesn't mean that they know them well. We will all connect with acquaintances but may not feel comfortable in facilitating the introductions, so if they decline to help it's probably not down to anything you have done.

Make LinkedIn part of a daily routine

You can't complete it and think this is it! At least a couple of times a week, update your status, read updates from your connections, read, and comment on discussions within groups you belong to, review your connections, see what they are doing and how you can help, identify jobs to apply for, and use LinkedIn to help with research.

Chapter Seven

CREATING YOUR MESSAGE, THE PERSONAL COMMERCIAL

T he first edition of this book included the chapter 'the personal commercial'. I've refocused this as the work you will do on creating a message that will be used in various situations, not just when you meet someone in person.

You need a clear message so that other people understand what you want and how they can help you. My introduction will be slightly different as I'm a consultant rather than someone seeking a job:

> *"Hello, my name is Denise Taylor. I'm a specialist career psychologist, working with individuals to help them understand themselves and identify a job that will match their skills, interests and talents. I then support them throughout their job search – in developing a CV, planning their campaign and helping them develop interview techniques. This is enhanced through my ongoing assignments as an assessment specialist helping to recruit graduates and professionals through assessment centre selection procedures." (75 words)*

This is sometimes called a personal commercial or an elevator speech. There are similarities with TV and radio commercials that (in 30 seconds) make you aware of a product.

When do I use this?

You can use this when you meet new people, while networking, at interview, or any time when people may ask you what you do. You can also use it in written communication such as the first paragraph of a letter or email, or at the start of your LinkedIn profile.

The format needs to be in clear, specific stages such as:

Example 1	Example 2
• Who am I?	• Name and job title
• What do I do?	• Desired position
• How do I help?	• Something unique
• What do I need?	

Here is an example:

THE 'WHO AM I' STAGE

The first step is to say who you are and what you do. This needs to be upbeat and positive. You don't want to come across as negative, so don't say things such as:

- I'm Fred Jones and I've been made redundant.

- I'm Christine Lewis and I'm an unemployed graduate.

In most case you will want to introduce yourself as an expert in a particular area, or at the very least to have something that makes you stand out from everyone else. Why not have a go?

I'm, _____, and my expertise is in _____

My name is _____. I am a specialist _____

I'm _____. I am specially trained in _____

My name is _____. I am a qualified _____

THE 'WHAT I DO' AND THE 'HOW YOU CAN HELP' PHASE

The second step is to say what you do and how you can help. This helps people to understand the details of your work. A job title is too distant. Will people really know what it means? I will say

> *"I work with individuals to help them understand themselves and identify a job that will match their skills, interests and talents. I then support them throughout their job search – in developing a CV, planning their campaign and helping them develop interview techniques."*

Some other examples:

- *"I create warm relationships with customers so they come back and buy from me again and again."*

- *"I am careful with my deliveries and make smooth and pleasant transactions for customers."*

- *"I can create passion for history in students by helping them understand how knowledge of the past can be applied in many situations and how the process of conflict has relevance today."*

Activity: Now you try:

I help _____

I create _____

I work with _____

THE 'WHAT YOU NEED' PHASE

The final step is to say what you need from them. If you are looking for people to help on your career quest, you need to be specific. Saying: *"I'm looking for a well-paid job,"* or *"I need security for the future,"* is far too broad. Similarly, to say *"I was a childcare worker,"* is too narrow. It's best to expand your statement to be more specific and to say you are looking for a job working with children in places like nurseries, hospitals or infant schools.

My job search clients may say:

- *"I'm looking to talk with people who can help me get a better understanding of the role of technical author."*

- *"I would like to explore the possibility of working as a TV researcher. Would you know someone I could talk with?"*

- *"I'm looking for accountants to discuss how to make the transition from marketing to finance. Could you suggest someone for me to talk to?"*

Now you try. What do you need from others? Make a note.

Now put it all together; write it down and say it aloud. Does it flow, does it sound right for you? When we draft things out, they often come across as stilted, so use less formal language. Now say this to family and friends and be receptive to feedback. Make any changes you need to make and create a second draft.

Congratulations! You have now created your personal message. Now review it and make sure that it avoids the 10 most overused buzzwords. Use a thesaurus and avoid the following:

1. Extensive experience
2. Innovative
3. Motivated
4. Results orientated
5. Dynamic
6. Proven track record
7. Team player
8. Fast paced
9. Problem solver
10. Entrepreneurial

Now that it's complete, you can use it in different ways:

- At an interview to answer the question, *"Tell me about yourself."* You will of course go into more detail – see the Interview section for more on this.

- In a cover letter to highlight your background and key abilities.

- When talking to other people to help you get contacts for information-gathering interviews.

- During any professional, social or organisational meeting when you are asked to introduce yourself.

- Cold-calling companies to explain how you may be of service.

Now that you have learned how to create your message, you can keep it up to date as you develop new roles.

You could also benefit from a longer version of this, something that could take 60 rather than 30 seconds. The structure of this could be

1. A short introduction of up to 10 seconds to include mentioning your name

2. Key background, 20 seconds

3. Interesting story, 20 seconds

4. Summary of what you seek, 10 seconds

Section 3

Finding Things Out

Effective job search involves finding things out – through informal connections with people, fact-finding interviews and online research. This section provides effective and easy to follow guidance on how to do all three.

Chapter Eight

NETWORKING – IT JUST MEANS TALKING TO PEOPLE!

You have probably heard that most jobs are filled through networking. This is getting a job offer through a recommendation, or through your name being put forward by someone who knows you. As I worked on this chapter I picked up the phone to Ruth who wanted to recommend me for a consultancy assignment. Ruth and I chat occasionally and we are both aware of each other's strengths; she knows my experience and background.

The same could happen for you; someone you know may be asked if they know someone with a particular background or skill set and next thing you are being interviewed.

Staying in touch with people should not be something that's only done when we need a job; it should be part of our career management strategy. But we don't always stay in touch with people and there are many people we say hello to (at the gym, the school gate, social meetings) who have no idea what we do or what we are looking for.

What is networking?

Networking is a means of making connections and is part of business life. It is an essential element of job search where you use relationships and contacts to help you to identify work opportunities. A vital feature of the process is for you to use your existing contacts to give you the names of other contacts, thereby widening your network.

Why a network is important

Building up your network of contacts is very important as it's a way of sharing ideas, gaining leads, following ideas and practising interviews.

Networking works! Research by the Chartered Institute of Accountants shows networking is very effective. Of those surveyed under the age of 35, a quarter got a job through networking; between the ages of 35 and 50 it was half, and for those over 50, 80% found their job through networking.

In a recession, where there are fewer jobs available it's even more important to get as many people as you can helping you with your job search – by letting you know of jobs that might be coming up, getting you introductions to people that can help, and keeping you updated on new initiatives.

Job offers don't always come through a direct contact, but through someone who knows a friend or colleague of a friend.

Who is in my network?

We all have a network – it's the people we know. There's the close network of family, friends and business colleagues, and the loose network of people we know through clubs and organisations (church, professional societies, trade associations), people from school and university, both friends and teachers, contacts from seminars and conferences, bank manager, accountant, local professional people, friends of your parents (or children), neighbours (past or present) and more.

It's useful to make a note of everyone you know; either set up a spread sheet or use the networking form in the additional resources folder on the website. Go beyond their name and include contact details too.

Each of the people you list has their own network, so telling your hairdresser that you are looking for a specific type of job could lead to her telling another client, and within 3 conversations someone knows about a company that might have an opening for someone like you. As we begin to network we find more people that we can talk with; why not talk to the person next to you in the queue at the petrol station, supermarket, etc?

I think it's less important to struggle to identify your top 10 contacts than simply getting the message out there. For example, let your friends on FaceBook know what you are looking for, and get a clear message out to everyone you meet. The previous chapter guides you in creating an effective message to use on Facebook and elsewhere.

You can expand your network through getting involved in a range of organisations. If you want to get back into Human Resources, go to the CIPD meetings, but any organisation where you meet people will be useful. Volunteering can introduce you to a new group of people, and someone may know someone who needs you! If you don't have access to a local professional meeting you could join the online option; most have a group on LinkedIn, plus there are other groups you can find via Yahoo and Google.

Keeping records

If you have set up a spreadsheet you can keep track of when you were in touch, and what you sent – an email, 1-page summary etc. You can also keep track of what you have done to help them – emailed an article etc.

A card box system is a low tech way of dealing with the data – one side of the card can contain contact details (names, email and phone numbers), who referred you, etc. The other side can detail the date of each phone call and/or meeting, topics discussed, and any personal insights.

Jibber-Jobber.com, created by Jason Alba, author of *I'm on LinkedIn, now what?*, could help you to keep track of everyone you meet, alongside everything you have shared, such as your CV or articles. You can also log answers to questions people ask you, and review the article library. There is a free version available.

Keeping in touch

It's important that you keep your contacts informed of your progress with the companies and people to whom you have been introduced. This will maintain their interest and keep you in mind as they come across further useful information or people.

Is it relevant to me?

Many people tell me that networking isn't relevant to them, only to 'high flyers'. However, once they understand the importance of talking to others to find jobs, they begin to network. For example, Vicki, who had just been made redundant from her job as a training administrator, found out about a small company who needed admin help and found herself on a shortlist of one. Alison's partner spoke to a Chief Executive of a company and found out about a job that would be perfect for Alison. This contact meant that Alison got seen and shortlisted.

Be ready to help others

It's not a one way process. You also need to look for ways that you can help somebody else. When you meet someone, especially at an event that's been set up for networking, you can develop relationships through asking questions about the challenges they face, and the help they need.

Before you make contact, get clear on what you want. If you are vague it's much harder to get help from others. Not just, *"I'm looking for something in the training field,"* but *"I'm a technical trainer looking for opportunities to teach end-users how to use business applications software in a Windows environment."* Certainly you need to go beyond the vague, *"I'm looking for anything"*:

- *"I've worked as a legal executive and now want to move into public relations."*

- *"I've been an occupational therapist, but am now looking for something in writing, such as on a newspaper, a magazine, or company newsletter."*

- *"I've 5 years' experience in managing an English department at grammar school, and I want to use my management skills within a customer service environment."*

- *"I'm a highly experienced accountant and want to work for a small company that wants an ethical and pragmatic accountant."*

Be specific. The more information you give, the easier it is for the other person to think of possible job opportunities and contacts that can help you.

It can also help if you suggest the types of companies that would be interested in you. For example, instead of saying, *"I was a nursery nurse,"* you could say, *"I'm looking for a job working with children in places like a nursery school, day care, hospital or primary school."*

So what will you say? Write down a first draft and read it out loud. Is it clear? Do you understand what you are looking for? Will others? If it's vague or complicated people are unlikely to help you.

> **It's easiest to network with people you already know. Bring them up to date on what you have been doing and what you want to do.**

People you know

If you haven't been in touch for a while, start by bringing them up to date with what you have been doing and then ask for what you want. If these are previous employers or customers you could ask them if they would be happy to provide a letter of recommendation, or a recommendation on LinkedIn. Getting them to think about your strengths may remind them how you could help out with a current project.

Offer to help them, find out what they need, and as you start talking to more and more people you may be able to help them too!

Richard felt uneasy in contacting people he had not spoken to in years just because he now had some self-interest. He bit the bullet and was pleasantly surprised – ex colleagues and friends were really pleased to hear from him. Talking to people was so much more helpful than online research. Meetings, often over lunch, explored options in detail, eliciting some honest appraisals of what he could and couldn't do, and what some of the roles REALLY involved. Richard said, *"The more I did this the more I had an idea on where I could employ my strengths."* His contacts were also keen to try to help out where possible. *"One ex-colleague told me he'd put me in front of anyone I wanted (in his sector), and to just be clear on what I wanted to do. Another got me involved in a short project for which I'm still employed. I still keep in touch with all those people I contacted."*

Networking should be part of your daily routine

You can meet people in person and via LinkedIn. Face-to-face meetings are generally best, but you can still create warm and effective meetings online.

Don't forget about using Friends Reunited to reconnect with old school friends; you may be surprised by what they are doing now and how you may be able to help each other.

Face to face meetings with people should be part of your daily routine, so make a note of the number of people you will contact each day. This provides you with a means of monitoring your progress. Plan to pick up the phone to 10 people, for example, and to meet with 2 people each day. You can then monitor your success.

It is essential to prepare thoroughly before each call. You may like to start with people you know quite well.

You must not ask for a job, but for advice. Ask for a job and the answer will almost always be no, but advice could lead on to details of a job. Ask for the names of other people to contact. You could also ask whether she or he sees the current needs of their company changing in the near future.

> People must want to recommend you. You may like to find out, possibly via someone else, what your friends and contacts think of you, and if there is anything that would stop them recommending you. No one is going to recommend anyone who could embarrass them through having an 'interesting personality' or being the sort of person that always moans.

Would you recommend *you*?

NETWORKING – A STEP-BY-STEP GUIDE

Demonstrate enthusiasm. So many employees moan about their job, so it can be a 'breath of fresh air' to talk with someone with well directed enthusiasm.

1 – Initial contact

Call or write to each person on your list. You can't just send a brief letter or email. You must include detailed and specific ideas about what you are looking for, and remind your contact of some of your key achievements. If this approach is because of a referral, be sure to mention the person's name.

Typical structure of a letter

Short introduction:

> *Despite the recession I'm determined to get a job and I'm researching to find out as much as I can so when I do apply I'll be a strong candidate.*

In the next paragraph, include what you are seeking and what you want:

> *I am looking for a project management position within the following companies (list the names of the companies here). Do you know anything about these companies, or know anybody who works for them? I've looked online but would love to know more about the management style, business plans, or anything you think may be useful for me.*

In the next paragraph, remind them of your skills and achievements. Make it simple for those who may not understand the specifics of your skills base. In the next paragraph, you could include a quote from one of your bosses/clients.

You can conclude with:

> *I'm really excited by the prospects of working in this area and would love to talk to anyone who might be able to help me.*

> *Thanks so much for your help, and I'd be very happy to send my CV to any of your contacts. I'll be in touch in a couple of days to arrange a time to meet.*

This can be a better approach than sending your CV straight away, and it gets you a chance to follow up with your contact.

> Whilst it can be interesting to meet for coffee or lunch, make sure there is a purpose to your meeting. Have a focus to the session; ideally you want to get a referral to someone who can help you.

2 – Schedule a face-to-face meeting

Make an appointment and arrange to meet your contact. You could suggest meeting before or after work. Some people can be hard to contact, but do persevere. Relationships build much more quickly when you meet face-to-face.

Primary contacts

Primary contacts are people you already know. If you haven't been in touch for a while, they will want an update on what you have been doing, so prepare some brief notes, covering:

- The reason for contact – you are or will be looking for a job.

- What you have done since you last met, in case it is needed.

- Details of your recent achievements at work.

- The areas or industries in which you are particularly interested.

- A prepared list of what you want from this contact, with space to write answers against each item. This could include information about any possible leads or information in the area or industries in which you are interested, information about specific requirements and names, or addresses and phone numbers of any contacts who can give further help along the lines of the above.

Referred contacts

Ask each person you contact if they know of anyone who might know of job opportunities in your field. If they give you a name, ask if you can mention their name when you contact the person they've recommended.

A primary contact may be willing to pick up the phone and introduce you to their contact, or to email your CV.

You will have to decide whether your initial contact is by phone, email or letter. A phone call will work well with someone you know, but you may not be able to get through to busy people. Sending a short letter followed by a phone call means that the person is expecting your call.

I don't recommend emailing someone you don't know as it's too easy for them to hit the delete key. You have a better chance of something being read if you post it or if it's forwarded by someone they know.

Networking Questions

As you make contact with people, the following questions may be helpful:

To a close friend or person who can give a positive recommendation:

- Can I use your name as a referee when I apply for positions?
- Could you write me an open letter of recommendation?

To any friend or acquaintance:

- Can you let me know if you do hear of any job openings?
- Do you know of anyone who works for ....?

To someone who works where you want to work

- Can you tell me what it's like to work here?
- Are there any vacancies?

To previous employers:

- Will there be job openings in the near future?

- Can you think of any other companies that may be recruiting people with my skills?

- Would you be able to write me a letter of reference?

- Would I be able to use you as a reference when applying for positions?

- When I contact that company, may I say that you suggested I contact them?

Ask everyone you can for specific information. For example, if you want a job in the computer gaming industry you could ask:

- What do you know about the computer gaming industry?
- Tell me about the business culture in Dundee?

- What companies would you suggest I contact?
- What are your thoughts about the proposed merger of A and B?
- Do you know anyone who works for Clink Productions?

WHY DO SOME PEOPLE FIND IT DIFFICULT TO NETWORK?

We can sometimes find that fear holds us back. This can be

- **Fear about networking**

  You are not the first or only person who needs to find another job. It is more than likely that some of your primary contacts will have shared the same experience or have a relation who has done so.

- **Fear of the unknown**

  This is nearly always based on the fact that people have not tried to network before or have done so once in a half-hearted way.

- **Fear of refusal**

  This has much in common with the second concern. People who have used networking in establishing and promoting themselves will tell you it is rare they get an outright rejection. The contact may not be able to give any useful advice or help but that is not rejection. Of course you will get some people who don't want to meet with you. It can help to use LinkedIn to build online connections with people you know less well. If you do get a refusal, don't take it personally, since you don't know the reason.

- **Fear of being judged**

  There may be a part of you that will be worried about what the other person will think of you. You may believe that they will judge you for your misfortunes – if, for example, you have lost your job. And maybe some people will. However, your real friends and allies will not. It's ok to be afraid. It is not ok to let the fear stop you.

- **Fear of being thought to beg or to seek charitable help**

  You are being an adult and asking for advice. Most people love to help others.

Richard told me he had fun networking and he has found it much easier to get people to read his CV as a result of 'touching flesh'. He's realised that research is best done by talking to people, not by emailing or trying to work it out alone. He said, *"For the senior level position I want, it's about trust and connections. That's what I'm working on."*

- **Fear of 'letting down' their contact**

  This is by turning out to be less capable than they have appeared. We can sometimes have negative feelings if we are getting low with our job search. One way to tackle this is to do something.

NETWORKING EXAMPLE

Jo had worked as a marketing executive in the telecoms industry. She was no longer happy in this work and there were talks of redundancy, so she was keen to make a move. Jo followed the exercises in this book, identified her skills and values, and this made her realise that it was the right job – she loved marketing but she felt she was marketing the wrong product. She was very keen to use her skills in the charity sector but wasn't sure how she would make the move.

She didn't know anyone who worked in the charity sector, but used her contacts to find people to approach. Within a week, she had the names and contact details of six people who worked for charities, including Charles. Charles was an operations director with a national charity, and had previously worked in marketing with a children's charity.

This is a typical letter. You can use it to form the basis of your own letter.

Dear Charles,

I would welcome input regarding the next phase of my career.

Having developed my skills and experience as a marketing executive in the telecommunications industry, I am considering transferring my skills to the not-for-profit sector.

You know a lot about the charity sector and I would appreciate hearing about its current conditions. I have enclosed my CV to bring you up to date with what I have been doing over the last few years and would appreciate meeting up with you soon.

I will telephone you in the next few days to find out when you are free.

Yours sincerely,
Jo Harvey

Jo sends out the letter so that it will arrive on a Tuesday (to avoid the Monday rush), and telephones on Thursday to make an appointment.

The phone call

As indicated in the letter, Jo follows this up with a phone call. She stands up to make her call as she will sound more alert.

"Hello, Bill Jones suggested I call you. I am doing research into charity marketing (name the company's business) and you are a well-regarded professional who really understands this sector. Could you spare 20 minutes at the end of the day to answer some questions?"

On the other end, the person asks, *"Are you looking for a job?"*

"Not yet. First I need to be sure that my skills will be needed in the charity sector and I am sure you can help me to understand this. Could we meet on Tuesday next week?"

Be prepared when networking by phone for questions about yourself, perhaps from a receptionist wanting to pass on a message to the person you want to contact.

3 – Conducting the meeting

You have requested the meeting so you must decide on the agenda and lead the discussion. Advance preparation is therefore essential, as it is for any kind of interview.

Start by establishing some rapport. If you are talking to a primary contact, remind him or her of the circumstances in which you became acquainted or have worked together. In the case of a referred contact, get him or her to talk about their business and the issues they currently face.

- Make it clear that you don't expect a job offer.

- Keep the meeting short, a maximum of 30 minutes.

- Be clear on what you want.

- Summarise your own background and situation and outline your job search strategy.

- Ask for comments on its viability within their sector and invite suggestions. If you have a target list of companies, she or he may be prepared to evaluate them or may know some senior people to whom they can provide an introduction.

- Get your contact to comment on your CV in relation to your job search, either during your meeting or by leaving/sending a copy. Ask them how your CV looks. What would they change about it? Does it make sense? Ask them if they know anyone you could talk to.

- The more she or he knows and understands about your background, the more they will be able to help, either in terms of additional contacts or the direction of your search. There is always the possibility that during your meeting, your contact will begin to consider you for a position within his or her own organisation – one clue being that the contact starts to take control and asks you questions.

Be careful not to talk too much

Listen 80%. Talk 20%.

Listen carefully to what they have to say. They may tell you about problems in their company or industry and you can then think about ways to solve them and get back in touch.

Let's see how Jo is getting on

At the meeting, Jo repeats the substance of the letter. Charles tells her useful facts about the present state of the industry. Jo doesn't ask for a job, but tentatively asks if any consultancy work is needed in Charles's organisation. Whether paid or initially unpaid, this might lead to a permanent job, full or part-time. She ends the meeting with:

> *"That's been really useful. From what you have said, I'd like to meet with some environmental charities. Can you let me have the names of two people who I can talk with in order to get more details about requirements there?"*

4 – Follow up

For Jo, the meeting has been positive and she sends out a handwritten note, rather than an email. Applying the personal touch helps create greater impact. She uses correspondence cards (size of a postcard) pre-printed with her name and contact details so the note is quick to produce.

> *Dear Charles,*
>
> *Thank you for talking with me yesterday. I found it very helpful. I appreciated your taking time out of your busy schedule to do this.*
>
> *With best wishes*
> *Jo Harvey*

5 – Getting a positive lead

Eventually a contact may say:

> *"Delighted to give you advice. Did you say that you know about abc? Our human resource people would like to talk to you about an opening we have here…"*

Often, the opening has not been advertised, and perhaps has not yet been fully defined.

Keep in contact after your job search is over

Now that you have taken the time to develop relationships with people in your network, you need to make sure you stay in touch. Contact the people who were unable to help as well and let them know how you have got on and thank them once again for their time. Look for ways to stay in touch at least a couple of times a year, and look for ways to pay the person back.

Go to professional meetings and conferences

Professional associations have monthly meetings and you get a chance to meet with people working in your chosen career area. Conferences can be a great way of being found and making connections. Since many can be expensive, perhaps you could volunteer. For helping delegates to register you should get free entry, so get in touch with the event organiser.

Online networking

Networking is a sociable activity – you are getting out there and meeting people. Not everyone finds this easy. If you are someone who is more introverted in nature, or who finds being with many new people a stressful experience, you may wonder what else you can do.

Although face-to-face networking is the most effective, you can start to connect with people online through contributions to discussion groups and forums, and being active on LinkedIn. There are many discussion groups out there and you can find lists at www.groups.google.com. There are also specific sites such as http://tinyurl.com/kom47 which comprises discussion groups and mailing lists of people specializing in specific aspects of medicine, pharmacy, pharmaceutical sciences and health-related issues.

On these sites, you won't want to go straight in and ask for a job. It's more about adding to your contacts list (while helping others on the forum). You need to get a feel for these sites before you comment (known as lurking), but do look for where you can add helpful comments enhancing your reputation. Many sites will allow you to add a signature line where you can add some personal details of yourself with your contact details clearly stated.

As you get to know someone online it makes it easier to pick up the phone or meet via Skype or face to face.

Visit the website to download the additional resources:

- *The formal networking event, audio.*
- *Networking form.*

Chapter Nine

FACT FINDING INTERVIEWS

If you are considering a change of career, or just getting started, the first step is to spend time online, gathering as much information as you can about your chosen field. This online research is a great step towards finding a new job. You can use websites and forums to find out about different jobs, entry requirements and career prospects (there's little point trying to get into an industry in decline).

Once you have pared your list down to a couple of jobs, you can move onto fact-finding interviews. The person you will want to speak with is likely to be someone with a busy schedule, therefore you must be prepared so you don't waste his or her time. Nothing is more infuriating than people asking questions they could have found answers to via web sites. Don't waste their time or yours!

Fact-finding interviews can be used to:

- Learn about a specific company – if you want to work for a large retail chain or a company like Innocent, how does your vision relate to the reality?

- Understand more about the specifics of a particular job – when you get beneath the job title, what will you be doing?

- Increase your chances of success with a job application – what can you find out that will help to customise an application?

You will find people to talk with via a 'cold call' or through people you know (or are known to people you know). We've already talked in *Chapter 8: Networking* about the need to develop a network of people you know. They may be doing the type of job you'd like to pursue, or may know someone who does.

Fact-finding interviews are a chance to really find out more about a particular job. You can move beyond what you have found online and ask more detailed questions to someone who does the job and can tell you about the negatives as well as the positives involved. You can also use this as a chance to find out about some of the challenges facing a particular industry. Finding out more about these areas will enable you to enhance an application.

WHILST THESE ARE CALLED FACT-FINDING INTERVIEWS, THEY SOMETIMES RESULT IN JOB OFFERS

After several fact-finding interviews, you could come across as someone who is already far more knowledgeable than most of the applicants people see at interview, and you may impress sufficiently to get a job offer. Of course, it's not the purpose of the meeting, but by asking pertinent questions, and discussing how you might consider your background and experience match your understanding of the job, you can appear as a very credible candidate.

Let's now talk you through what you need to do.

Step 1: Identify who to talk with

You can arrange for fact finding interviews by a referral, an introductory letter or a cold call. The previous chapter on networking will help you identify and find people who can help. You can also find out details of particular companies through research (see Chapter 10).

If you have read an interesting article, you could contact the author and make reference to this. Make the link between what you have read and your career research.

Step 2: Questions to ask

Being able to ask questions of someone in a particular industry is a great opportunity, so choose your questions carefully. What do you really want to know? What kind of information is most important to you? You may choose to start with some general questions then pinpoint certain areas with more specific questions. The longer you speak with someone, the more detailed you can become. You'll find that the more people you interview, the more you'll know what to ask.

A fact finding interview usually lasts for a maximum of 30 minutes, so plan your questions in advance. You should pare down your list to 10 at the most. The following questions will be a good start. Download a document containing these and more via the downloads page.

- *What do you do during a typical workday or week?*

- *What kind of challenges or problems do you have to deal with in this job?*

- *What skills make you good at what you do?*

- *What do you find most satisfying and most frustrating about your job and field?*

- *What do you see as the future for this kind of work?*

- *What preparation, training and/or experience would you suggest for someone entering this field?*

- *What are alternative routes for entry into this field?* (if you don't have an MSc, for example).

- *What would I need to do to become an attractive candidate for a job in this field?*

- *Who else would you recommend or suggest I talk to in order to learn more about this career?* (Don't forget to ask them to phone these people on your behalf.)

- *May I contact you if other questions arise?*

Some of these questions may require quite a bit of reflection and thought from the person being interviewed, so consider sending the questions in advance.

Step 3: Arrange an appointment

You will have to decide whether your initial contact is by phone, email, LinkedIn message or letter. Sending a short message and following it up with a phone call works well. That way, the person is expecting your call, and if they are not available, they may have left a message with their assistant.

Whichever approach you choose:

- Clearly state your purpose. Be brief, concise and explain your interest in the company or field.

- Reinforce that you are not looking for employment. You are seeking advice and information.

- Take responsibility for making contact. Follow up with a call to set up the appointment. It is often best to call after 5 p.m. when assistants may not be at their desks.

- Email is quicker and cheaper but it is too easy for your email to be deleted. A posted letter has greater impact.

Here is an example letter:

Dear Mr Johnstone,

I have spent a great deal of time researching different careers of interest to me, and determining which will play to my strengths and abilities. I have already undertaken some online research and would appreciate meeting with someone who is experienced in this area to find out further information.

Would you be able to give me just 20–30 minutes of your time to gather information and obtain some advice about pursuing a career in land surveying? If you believe a colleague would be more appropriate to speak with, perhaps you could help me contact them.

I will phone on the afternoon of Tuesday, 26th April to discuss a convenient time to meet.

I really appreciate your taking the time to read this letter, and I look forward to talking with you.

Yours sincerely

Be sure to follow up the letter with a phone call to arrange the appointment. The person you contact will be busy, so ask again for just 20–30 minutes of their time and make sure you don't linger on the phone. Being brief and to the point demonstrates your professionalism. A sample phone script is:

> *"Hello Chris, This is Jane Robinson. I sent you a letter a couple of days ago in which I wrote about my interest in working as a land surveyor. I've done extensive research online and now need to talk with someone who is able to answer some questions and provide feedback on my approach.*
>
> *Could we schedule a 20–30-minute meeting? I'm happy to talk in person or by phone, whichever is most convenient for you."*

Or you could phone direct, which is a 'cold call', using these two examples to help you create your own version.

> *"Hello, my name is Jane Robinson. I was given your name by Denise Watson who thought you may be able to give me some advice.*
>
> *I'm researching different careers and have yet to start a serious job search. I'm considering a career within market research. Whilst I don't have any previous direct work experience, my online research has identified that I have many transferable skills. I'd like to find out more if my background could be of use in this area.*
>
> *Could we arrange to talk for 20 minutes to enable me to ask you a few questions? I'd be happy to meet at a time and place to suit you or we could meet via Skype."*

An alternative start could be:

> *"Good morning, I am currently a .... with expertise in ... I'm very interested in making the move into project management and I would appreciate meeting with you to find out how credible a candidate I would be, and what I may need to do to enhance an application."*

When you call, be ready to ask your questions on the phone then and there. It's not ideal, but often people want you to go ahead and ask your questions.

Sometimes people think you are looking for a job with them. If they ask, reassure them that you are not. Stress that you are doing research into this particular career to judge your own suitability. These sorts of calls can be a bit stressful the first time you do them, so consider doing a trial run with someone you know and have them comment on your approach and style.

> You must do the follow up call. If you wait for them to contact you, it just won't happen!

When you make the call, stand up! It keeps your energy high so you sound confident. And breathe! If you haven't spoken to anyone that day, talk out loud to yourself; it will stop you having a dry mouth.

When you ring, you'll probably get through to their PA/secretary, so politely ask to speak to the person you have written to. You can truthfully say that they are expecting your call as you wrote to arrange this.

End the call by thanking them and confirm the date and time for your meeting. You can email a note of thanks and confirm the appointment in writing.

Of course you won't get a meeting with everyone you contact. Before the recession, the success rate of my clients was between 30 and 70%. If you are pleasant and not pushy, you will have some success getting appointments. If not, take a good look at your approach. Are you emphasising your candidacy for a job rather than your research into it?

Step 4: The meeting

You have done well to get this meeting, so make good use of your time. Take along your list of questions and listen carefully to everything they have to say.

- Again, make sure the interviewer knows you are seeking advice, NOT a job.

- Show them that you value their time by being prepared. Your questions could include finding out the likelihood of any suitable jobs being advertised in the near future, and where the jobs would be advertised.

- Ask for feedback on your CV, qualifications and proposed direction.

Prepare a list of companies the interviewer may know, and ask for advice and opinion as to whether you would fit in to these organisations. Ask for contacts who could help with advice and suggestions (NOT to request jobs from) and ask for introductions, written or personal. Always make sure you have permission from the interviewee to use their name as part of the introduction to the person to whom they refer you.

If you are asked questions, make sure you do not express negative views about previous organisations you have worked for. Ask permission to keep the person you interviewed informed of the progress you make.

> You went there for advice. Make sure you get it!!

You could end the meeting with something like:

> *"I've learned a great deal today. Having seen your organisation, I'm interested in talking to more people in this field. I'm especially interested in (any special area that came up during your meeting). Whom do you think I should talk with next?"*

Or

> *"I really appreciate all of your time and effort today. Now that I've seen the career closely, I feel that I might be more effective in a smaller organisation where I will not be called upon to specialise quite so much. At least I need to find out. Whom do you think I should talk with next?"*

Be sure to phrase it that way. It's positive and assumes that they know someone (as opposed to asking *"Can you think of anyone I should talk with next?"*). You may find they give you a name or number, and possibly pick up the phone to make an appointment for you.

Follow up with a thank you note. You can keep the connection open by offering them something of value, such as a copy of a useful article you found through your research.

Step 5: Review

The final step is to review what you have learned and determine what you will do next time. Consider both the important information you gathered and how you came across. Then ask yourself how you can improve for next time.

Keep a summary of what you have found out and add it to your file. You may like to keep details on their name, position, company, meeting summary, how to get started, further people to contact etc. You can access a form via the downloads page.

Through your discussions you may realise that a particular career path doesn't interest you. Don't be discouraged; this is a good outcome and means you won't waste time pursuing an unfulfilling career. You can still follow up and say that having spoken to them you are now more interested in exploring, for example, other career options in the same or a different field. Then define that new direction and ask for advice or referrals.

As you find out more, you should become much clearer on the jobs and industries you have researched. Then you can focus on a specific job or a combination of two interests. For example, if you are interested in both engineering and music, or food and research, find out about careers that integrate both passions.

Visit the website to download the additional resources:

- Fact finding interviews, list of questions.
- Contacts summary sheet.

Chapter Ten

RESEARCH FOR JOB SEARCH

Research is needed at different stages of job search, to find out what job(s) to apply for so you can enhance an application and be prepared for an interview.

SOURCES OF HELP

We all use Google, but people often miss out on the many ways it can be used in research.

ADVANCED GOOGLE

Apart from the most well-known job sites, you can also research specialist boards, some of which you may only find by doing an in-depth Google search. The typical Google search involves putting a word or phrase in the search bar but you can use search syntax to help further. If you want to be a marketing executive in Bristol, in the Google search bar you enter (~jobs OR ~careers) 'Marketing executive' Bristol.

You will then find specific jobs from a range of agencies. The first part of this search tells Google that you are seeking web pages that contain words related to either 'jobs' or 'careers'. By putting these words in brackets it makes it clear to Google that you want pages with either of these words. I've just done this and there are masses of options, but a quick run through the first 3 pages has identified a number of jobs I could apply for.

The second part tells Google the job that you seek. By putting this in quotes it means that you want these two words to appear together separated by a space. The final part shows the location.

You can get extensive help in searching Google from its website. Use the advanced search link and choose advanced search tips. Here's the

---

direct link: http://bit.ly/Gsearch. It leads to extensive help to create better searches.

Google has many options to help with your research, including Google finance: www.google.co.uk/finance. You can look at market news and a range of data related to a particular company.

GOOGLE ALERTS

Once you have found some really great searches you can save them as alerts and have new pages sent to you as they occur. You can set an alert at http://google.co.uk/alerts.

Business Library

Don't forget about the resources available at your county business library. In this you will have access to many helpful resources including

- Company information, not only addresses, but also performance and structure.

- Product information, who makes what, and where it can be bought.

- Market research information.

- Directories of key personnel in major companies.

- Information on business practice and developments.

The librarian will be able to help identify the most relevant books to use, such as BRAD Directories and Annuals or Current British Directories, Britain's Privately Owned Companies, Kelly's Business Directory and Key British Enterprises and Kompass.

Annual Reports

All public companies have to produce annual reports; you may be able to get copies from companies by contacting their Public Relations Departments. You can also access the latest Accounts and Balance Sheets, on payment of a fee, from the Registrar of Companies and Limited Partnerships, at Companies House.

There are many more online links, such as Factiva (a news database), the Financial Times, Hemscott (with details on quoted UK companies), Kompass online and more. Access links to these sites via the web site.

LABOUR MARKET INFORMATION

Labour market information (LMI) is obtained from a wide range of sources including government departments, sector skills councils, and local government. You can access up-to-date information from the Next Steps website using this link http://bit.ly/LMinfo. Before you spend too much time researching how to move into a new industry, you will want to confirm that jobs are likely to be available. Through LMI you could find that the median age is high and that many people are likely to retire in the next few years so more jobs may become available, or it may predict whether a particular job is likely to be outsourced.

WHEN TO RESEARCH

Clarify what job(s) you are going to apply for

The government site, Next Steps (http://bit.ly/profile4) has a comprehensive database of job profiles. This is a simple site to help you find out more about different jobs grouped into categories such as Administration and Clerical, Legal Services, Science and Research. This enables you to see if you have a background that will make it reasonably easy to make the move, or indicate the development you will need to be a credible candidate.

An alternative approach is to look at job sites, enter your key skills and see which jobs come up in the search. Some sites are hybrids of the two. For example, visit Target Jobs at http://bit.ly/targetjobs; follow their exercises and they will identify jobs which you can then explore on their site.

As you narrow down your options, you can use online sites with videos of job profiles. For example, Careers Box at http://bit.ly/careersbox.

You may find relevant information on the reality of a job through a site such as thejobcrowd.com where people will provide candid reviews of their jobs. This site is aimed at graduates, and details of other useful sites will be added to the website.

Researching the specifics of a job

As you identify a job to apply for, start to look at the job ads and identify the most common characteristics. You can then ensure that these keywords and qualities are used in both your CV and any communication (letter or email) you send to an employer.

To find recruitment consultants

One useful site is www.askgrapevine.com/jobs/a-to-z/ which provides details of recruitment consultants to enable you to identify the most relevant ones to approach.

Research when looking for companies to directly approach

You can find out about a company that may be expanding through reading the business press, reading about who is moving into new premises etc. As well as seeking a suitable role, job advertisements are a useful source of intelligence for your job search campaign. Don't just look for jobs you could do; notice if higher-level posts are being advertised, then jobs lower down in the organisation might become available.

Before a fact-finding interview

Value the person's time by finding out as much as you can online before you talk. There is nothing more likely to frustrate someone who has given up 20–30 minutes of their time than to have someone asking questions that were easily available online. It gives a negative impression and you have wasted an opportunity.

Getting in touch

If you want to apply for a job within a particular company but don't know who to contact, then you need to find someone who can help you. For example, if you are an electrical engineer, you can make contact with an accountant with that company and ask them questions. You can say something such as:

> *"I'm really interested in working with XYZ company as a media executive. Would you be able to suggest the right person for me to talk with about this career path?"*

> *"As someone who has worked with the XYZ company for 4 years, can you suggest ways I could make a speculative application stand out from many others?"*

> *"I have an interview scheduled next week with the XYZ company, could you let me know more about what it's like to work with your company and, in particular, details about the company culture?"*

I would of course include something about appreciating their time, but I want this to be something you write, that demonstrates the research you have already undertaken.

You may wonder if people will take the time to reply, but if you write a personal message, that is not just a direct lift form something that you have read, you are likely to find that many people are willing to help you. Of course you won't get success with every person you contact, so review the progress you make and look for ways to make your contact stronger.

To find out about the company

To increase your chance of success you need to do advanced research. Find out as much as possible about the company's needs, their problems and how you can solve them.

Once you know you want to work for a particular company, you can search via LinkedIn for people who used to work for it. Now they have left the company they are likely to be candid in the information they share.

Research will enable you to

1. Understand both the organisation and its industry and to ask intelligent questions demonstrating your knowledge at interview.

2. Find out if the company has a good reputation and is financially sound. This could be vital if you are giving up a secure job and want to know if the new organisation is likely to be safe.

For too many people think a quick look at the company website counts as research. This is the bare minimum, you need to do much more including finding forums to access customer comments. Through your research you should be able to answer the following questions:

The company

- Name of CEO and board members.

- The financial status of the company including sales and revenue for the current year, previous year and trends. How do this year's results compare with those of the last 3 years?

- Range of products, goods or services – what exactly does this company do?

- The views of its customers, suppliers, distributors, competitors and financial institutions.

- Key successes over the past year.

- Key challenges for the coming year.

- Recent company news.

- Primary competitors – how are they doing in comparison?

The Industry

- Major industry trends – what impact will they have?
- Will government initiatives create or decrease opportunities?
- Areas of opportunity?

Research 'the name'

Once you have identified a company, you want to find a particular person to write to. You could phone, or look on the company website and on LinkedIn. Phone the company to check, as the website may not be up to date. If you can't get the name through phoning reception/switchboard, you could call in the evening, say about 8.30pm, and get the security guard. Say you have a meeting with the marketing manager tomorrow and you need to check the name – this should get a result!

Once you have a name, search for it and the company in Google, this time using the News option. This will pull up any mentions in the press, or articles, conferences attended etc. Such information is very useful as it means you can start your letter by referring to what you have read.

To create a targeted CV and cover letter

Once you have done your research and identified the role you seek, such as project manager within the automotive industry, you can research to revise your CV and create a targeted cover letter. Your research should include identifying keywords used for a particular job. You can then ensure that these keywords are included in your CV, online applications etc.

Before an interview

The question, *"What do you know about us?"* is very common. As an interviewer, and talking with colleagues, we often note how many candidates appear not to have done any preparation. This is a key concern, so take time to find out about the company and the industry. The more senior the position you are aiming to obtain, the more important the research becomes.

Employers want applicants who have had the initiative, courtesy and enthusiasm to find out something about the organisation. Stand out by showing you have gone beyond a review of their website.

Back in January 2003 when I wrote my first version of this chapter, there were 5 companies interested in taking over Safeway, so if your application had been to a supermarket or a supplier to supermarkets, you may have wanted to consider the implications and be ready for questions on this area. You can also introduce the subject in your questioning at the end of the interview if it has not been referred to, thus demonstrating your initiative.

You will find links to many articles and references. Read what is being said in the business press and public views on open sites, and print it out so you can refer to it again. Be careful how you use this at interview – a reference to a highlighted comment to use as a question is one thing, but bringing out a file full of information you have collected may seem a bit bizarre.

Use forums

There are many forums, including Wikijob at www.wikijob.co.uk. From here you can look at forums, so if you were shortlisted for a job with Mercer, for example, you could chat and get details on other people's experiences. There are many other forums, and a Google search will find those relevant for you.

Next time you go for an interview armed with all relevant information, knowing who you are seeing, what the company does and who its competitors are, you will feel more confident and have a better sense of what you are letting yourself in for!

Visit the website to download the additional resources:

• Links to useful websites to use for research.

Traditional Job Search

The traditional way of finding a job is to look for one that's been advertised, and then to apply. However, this is the most competitive way of finding a job, so you need to create high-quality applications based on comprehensive research. This section will guide you in creating effective applications, cover letters and how to get the best out of working with recruitment agencies.

Chapter Eleven

FIND AND APPLY TO JOB ADS

Are you a job hunter who spends hours looking for jobs online? You are keeping busy but it doesn't mean that you are being effective. You need to limit your time using this approach as it is probably the least effective way of getting a job.

This chapter explains everything you need to do to increase your chance of getting shortlisted. There is a structured way to respond to job ads, and it's easy once you know what to do. Too many people think that they can use a similar application to all companies, but you need to specifically focus on what's included in the job advert. If you follow the steps in this chapter, your application will be much clearer and have a greater chance of success.

Finding job ads used to be so much easier: you read the relevant press and found the vacancies. Now there are literally thousands of sites with jobs, from the large sites like Monster, government sites such as Job Centre Plus, Aggregator sites such as Indeed.com, and many specific sites for specialist areas such as The Grocer.

If you find a job, you then have a choice:

1. Fully research the job and create a highly targeted reply.
2. Upload your generic CV and standard cover details.

Many times I hear of people who apply for 100+ jobs a week. The only way they can do this is if they are using option 2. This approach leads to rejection; they feel despondent but they carry on with this approach week after week.

Stop applying for anything you can only barely do and **start focusing on jobs where you match the requirements**. Take the time to apply properly. Stop wasting your time applying for jobs you have no chance of getting.

FINDING JOB ADS ONLINE

Almost every job ad is now found online. The most popular sites are large ones like Total Jobs, Monster, and Fish 4 Jobs. However, if *you* find a job ad there, so do many others, and it's not unknown for an ad to lead to well over a thousand applications.

Many of the advertised jobs don't even exist, or are already filled. Some jobs are placed by recruitment consultants who are trawling for CVs for their database. Others have been filled but remain posted on the site to gather more applicants to add to a database or as a form of marketing.

It's expensive for a company to place an ad on these sites so they will often choose a specialist site. These should prove more useful as they work hard to target their specific niche. Niche boards are built around an industry, geography, or job type, and enable more effective use of your time and efforts than would one of the major job sites. It's worth reviewing these niche sites to get a feel for the sorts of jobs that are being posted. If few are posted for a particular job group then you may be better looking in a different direction.

As you start your job search, identify 2 or 3 sites that are specifically targeted at your profession or location. For example if you are looking for a job in the not-for-profit sector, look at the jobs listed on www.jobsgopublic.com and http://jobs.thirdsector.co.uk.

If there is a professional journal associated with your targeted job, make sure to visit their website to find relevant jobs.

Also look on the websites of companies that interest you; their careers section will list any vacancies they have.

KEY TIPS

Set aside a limited amount of time each day for finding job ads to apply for. You must focus on the ones that will use your skills, not shoot in the dark at anything that remotely appeals.

Job Boards – Your details are prioritised according to date order, so go through and make a minor change each week to bump your details up the search results.

When you visit a site for the first time you can go back and look at job ads for up to 4–6 weeks earlier; the vacancies may not have been filled BUT do check they are still open vacancies before applying.

OTHER PLACES TO FIND JOB ADS

You can also look at the classified ads in newspapers; many smaller companies will post job ads in them.

Not all jobs are advertised in the press and online. Yesterday, as I drove into my nearest town, I passed job ads at a Simply Food store, a BP garage and an independent garage; an assistant manager job was advertised at a wine store, and vacancies at all levels were advertised in my dentist's and in store at Aldi.

REGISTERING ON JOB SITES

CAUTION!

Be careful before posting your details on job sites. Generally, you have to register by providing personal details and receiving a password. You want to be clear who will have access to this data. On some sites, 'employers' can access the site for free or a very low cost, hence the need to check on the security of your information.

There are many fake sites which are set up as a means of harvesting emails and personal details, and some have names very similar to genuine sites. Before you enter any personal details, do a Google search and read what people are saying about the site. Make sure there is a contact number and actual business address for the site, and find out about the security of your data.

Check to see if there is a privacy policy explaining what they do with your information. Read it carefully and print out the Privacy Policy and Terms of Use on the date you first use the site. Then monitor it for changes on a regular basis.

Carefully review the site before signing up. You need to check it has jobs of interest to you before registering your profile or CV.

- **Check if you can post more than one version of your CV on the site** so you can focus on different strengths for different jobs. Make a note of the version of your CV that you upload.

- **Can you delete your CV** once you have found a job? You don't want your new employer to think you are already looking for a new job. Keep a note of where you post your CVs so you can go back and remove them.

- **Is the site easy to navigate?** You have better things to do with your time than to struggle navigating through a site. You should find it easy to search for job and location. If not, move on to a site that suits you better.

Be sure that you can conceal your identity and are able to protect your contact information. On some sites, you can restrict the amount of personal information you share (a potential employer has to contact you via the site, not directly). It may slow down the process of getting in touch with you but it will also show you as someone with a good job to protect and someone who understands internet security.

Some sites allow you to see how many people have looked at your CV so you can know the number of companies that have and haven't contacted you. Use this information to help you review the information you have uploaded.

CHOOSE A CYBER-SAFE CV

Remove your standard contact details and replace them with a web based email address such as Hotmail, Yahoo or Gmail. Change your current company name to a more generic company description.

Make minor changes to your uploaded CV at least once a week to keep your details towards the top of a recruiters search.

SHORT-LISTING JOB ADS

As you review different websites, look at the jobs they advertise and compare these with your skills to see which jobs you are likely to get shortlisted for. Notice how the same job may be named by different titles. For example, if you want to work in HR, relevant jobs may be listed as HR Officer, Personnel Officer, HR Advisor, HR Adviser, Human Resources Advisor, Human Resources Adviser, HR Business Partner etc.

On most sites you can set up job alerts. You define the jobs you are looking for in terms of keywords, salary, location, etc. and will be notified of any vacancy that meets your criteria. Use your analysis of job ads to ensure that you include the keywords on your CV and in the details you upload.

On some sites you can enter a list of skills to see what jobs appear. You could do this with combinations of skills to see how this affects their selection. Ideally you will then shortlist jobs where there are lots of vacancies to increase your chance of success.

Richard said, *"I have tended to use skills such as 'project management' and 'consultancy' which can be applied across many different fields. Once you get an initial list, you can then refine it using more specific terms, e.g. training or e-learning. I've used this approach on The Guardian site and on Job Site."*

Keep track of the sites you are registered at and the alerts you create to make it easy to cancel them when you no longer require them.

Analysing the ad

Read the job ad carefully and highlight the key requirements so you can compare how well you match up.

There may be more details available via the company web site or by calling for more information.

If there is limited information available, demonstrate initiative and contact the company or recruitment consultant for more information. Gather as much information as you can. This is just the start of your research, and there is much more you can do – read the Research chapter for more details.

You can also find out more through using LinkedIn; ask a question to gather more information.

A Suggested Approach

In a buoyant market you could well apply for jobs where you only match 70%, but with the current situation, employers are looking for as close to a perfect match as possible. This doesn't mean that you can't apply but you have to be very careful to provide specific examples of what you can offer.

- Go through the job ads and identify those whose requirements you closely match. Print out and highlight the key points in the advert.

- As preparation, list these in a table with space to provide examples on the right; compare your skills and experience with those required. Confirm that you are a close or perfect match. If you don't meet the essential criteria you can still go ahead and apply but your chances of being shortlisted are slim.

- Analyse what the company or advertiser is looking for. Read between the lines. See if you have any other skills or experience which could be offered. What skills do you have relating to the job requirements, which may not be specified in the advertisement? They could well be of interest to the prospective employer. Use your initiative; indicate these in your letter of application if you believe they apply.

- How much more can you find out? You must do your research.

We can't treat your application in isolation from your cover letter. Both need you to identify each of the key requirements of the job and highlight how you match up. For example, if the job description requires someone with great organisational skills, you must highlight on your CV a job or a project in which you demonstrated your strengths in organisation. If it stresses the need for leadership qualities, include details of when you displayed your leadership skills.

Matching strengths and experience with the requirements of the job ad helps in shortlisting. Also think about other skills or experience you have relating to the job requirements (which may not be specified in the advertisement but may be of interest to the prospective employer).

Also, just for your benefit, make a note of any weaknesses that might be picked up on, such as lack of experience in the particular industry sector. How will you respond if challenged on this area?

Let's start with an example to show what's required.

List the key requirements in the job ad down the left and how you match up on the right.

Purchasing Manager

Purchasing Manager Main Duties	My Skills
Assist in the project 'gateway' governance process.	I am very familiar with the concept of project milestones and authorisation levels including the iterative process of projects.
Produce and manage procurement reports at all stages plus recommendations.	Structured documented communication at all stages of the procurement process with qualified proposals.
Project controls adhered to at all times.	Active management with appropriate action as required.
Project orders delivered on time, to agreed scope and on budget.	Expediting, management and financial control are areas in which I excel.
Manage the Shanks SC framework plus implement regular reviews.	Familiar with operating within a prescribed process with reviews weighted in accordance with the level of strategic/ operational risk.

Assist with project scopes and tenders plus participate in the selection of suppliers and contractors.	Experienced with working in cross functional teams to develop specifications and budget parameters plus evaluation and selection of the most suitable suppliers and contractors.
Ensure project procurement admin is undertaken.	Attention to detail and the completion of supporting documentation is critical for perceived and actual project success.
Evaluation of projects to capture lessons learned and best practice.	Best practice should be applied and evaluated to make further progress – lessons learned and incorporated as soon as project completed.

In the next chapter we will use this approach to create the cover letter.

Make sure your CV matches the job ad

Include extra detail in your CV where appropriate. For example, if the job asks for five years' sales experience in computer or related industry, your previous job as area sales manager becomes *"six (a specific number) years' experience as area sales manager for computers, laptops and printers"*. Describe your experience with concrete words rather than vague descriptions. For example, it's better to use *"managed a team of software engineers"* than *"responsible for managing, training…"*

For a big company, highlight your experience working for large businesses. For a smaller company, show how you can transfer your skills to a niche player, how you can work in a small team, and how you are happy to muck in when there is time pressure.

Sometimes we know we will be a great match for the job but our background seems better focused on something else. Address this in your cover letter and the top summary on your CV. Also make sure that your CV includes your most relevant achievements in a prominent position.

APPLYING FOR JOBS

Follow the instructions in the ad, it may say to send in your CV or you may need to complete an online form. If you need to phone for an application form, you don't have to get into a discussion, just leave your details while sounding friendly and upbeat.

If asked to ring for an informal chat, you are likely to get into a conversation that could be a screening discussion. Before phoning, do some careful preparation. Study the advertisement and list how you meet the required qualifications and experience. If possible, download any information and read it thoroughly in advance of the call, so you come across as someone who has thought through the role and has a good grasp of what the position entails. You can ask about:

- The kind of person they are looking for

- The organisational culture

- Reporting lines

- Types of people you will work with

- Key priorities

ONLINE APPLICATIONS

Many firms want you to provide answers to additional questions. I once worked with a client applying for a job with Innocent. Alongside uploading a CV, an applicant also needed to answer the following questions (I've provided a tip on how to answer the 5 questions listed below):

1. **You'd never know it but I can** ... something quirky to make you stand out.

2. **Tell us your reason for wanting to work at Innocent and the role in question. Why is this the right job for you?** ... link answer to details in the job.

3. **We love meeting people who leave things a bit better than they find them. So please tell us about a recent situation where you**

took the initiative and made something happen … use the STAR technique to structure your answer (see more in chapter 18).

4. **We're looking for people who face challenges head-on and deliver against the odds; what achievement are you most proud of?** … you need to expand and say WHY, this would be specific to yourself.

5. **We're especially interested in the stuff that you are passionate about, the things that make you tick. What gets you excited?** Create a reply that makes you come across as interesting.

Another unusual question you could be asked is something like this which was included on an application form for an Innovation Consultancy: *"If I was stuck next to you on a plane for 8 hours, what would my impression of you be?"*

Completing application forms

It's much easier to send off a fairly generic CV and cover letter. Completing an application form can take a lot of time. However, a generic CV and letter are unlikely to get you shortlisted, and once you have completed a couple of application forms you will find you have much of the information you need and you can cut and paste information into future applications.

> Always keep details of what you include in online forms so you can use them again.

Why do organisations use application forms?

Organisations use application forms for two main reasons: they make it quick and easy to compare applications since the information is presented in a standard way. Recruiters have to 'hunt' for information from CVs. Secondly, an application form can seek answers to specific details which are usually omitted from CVs and cover letters such as health, reasons for leaving jobs, etc.

Application forms are mainly completed online, so prepare your answers as a text document and cut and paste the information into the form.

First steps to completing the application form

Read the instructions carefully before you start. Make sure you understand what information is needed and where. When you complete an application form, your CV is usually not required, so if they don't ask you to send it, don't. Follow their instructions to the letter.

Keep in mind the requirements of **this** particular job. That's why an initial analysis is helpful. It means you can highlight previous work experience that relates to the job you are applying for.

It sounds obvious, but put the information in the correct boxes. The layout of forms is not standard and people will regularly fail to put the required details of previous jobs in the right columns. Occasionally you may not have anything to include (e.g. a professional membership). In this case, write N/A (not applicable) rather than leave it blank. Otherwise it looks like you missed the question.

With electronic forms, the gaps may increase as you type. But sometimes the space to write in is fixed, so think carefully about what to include and exclude. You may be limited to, say, 300 words for a particular question. Do your best to stay close to the limit.

Some questions will require brief, factual answers. Others will seek a narrative reply. Your responses should be drafted and redrafted before the relevant part of the original application form is finalised. If you are asked to name referees, make sure you ask them before listing their names.

Additional information section (also known as the personal statement)

Usually there will be a section for you to provide further information in support of your application, similar to what you would include in a cover letter. This is often the section that interviewers read most carefully. Make sure you include information on why you want the job and what makes you the right candidate. Stress your strengths, experience and achievements.

Imagine you are asked at interview *"Why should we appoint you?"* Your answer to that question could be all the things to be brought out in the open-ended section.

Strengthen your application by stating a key reason you applied for the job, and back it up immediately with an example. If possible, use terms from the advertisement for your key reasons. Continue for two or three key points, substantiating each general statement with an example. This can make your application very persuasive and penetrating.

If there are gaps in your career details (time out for study, family care, travel, etc), give an account of them on your form. Unexplained gaps are quickly spotted by the trained reader and can undermine your application.

The very best way to tackle this section is to use the advert, job description and person specification, and use each point as a sub heading with a specific example for each, just as when creating a cover letter.

Competency-based application forms

Competency-based application forms may appear complicated but they are a very structured approach to selling yourself. The competences cover the key skills or personal qualities needed for the job. These are like written versions of interview questions. For example:

Please provide an example of how you have demonstrated leadership.

> *"The young people who live in my village were interested in having a village skate park. Although there was discussion, nothing was happening so I volunteered to take charge. I gathered views on the subject, found out people's concerns, and then highlighted the benefits of a skate park for young people, and also discussed possible problems and how we could address them. I encouraged the young people to raise money and also submitted a bid for funding. The skate park is now in place, it's well used and I'm pleased to say there hasn't been any trouble."*

An alternative approach is to be asked to provide a specific example of one of the core competencies. You should be given instructions for how to respond. Because the instructions can vary from company to company, pay careful attention to their requirements. Let's look at a couple of examples:

Describe an effective team of which you are a member. What is your particular contribution to the team? In what way is the team effective?

> *"I have been a member of a local cricket club in Cheshire for the last two years, which not only is fun but also provides me a chance to keep fit and healthy. I am an important member of the team as I am the*

main strike bowler and sound middle-order batsman with an average of over 20 last season. I was therefore, partially responsible for one of the clubs most successful seasons in its history. In addition to good performances on the field, the club also performed well off the field, as we organised various fundraising events that have benefited both the club and the community. For example, this year we held a fete where I was responsible for running a food stall, which improved my organisational and interpersonal skills."

Describe a situation where you had to persuade someone to do something. How did you go about it? Were you successful?

"During the Duke of Edinburgh's Award scheme I led a group that improved the habitats and facilities of the Country Park at Marbury, Cheshire. It was often necessary to motivate a member of the team to start a new project or work in unfavourable weather conditions. Past experience of captaining the school rifle shooting and tennis teams has shown that the most effective method of persuading someone to do something was to confront them and persuade them of the wisdom of my proposals. There was an instance during the Duke of Edinburgh's Award scheme where a person did not want to begin the construction of a footpath as it was getting late. As his participation was essential and his negativity could have had a damaging effect on group morale, I drew on past experiences and persuaded him to continue working and the group made excellent progress."

You can read more examples on the website.

Submitting CVs and applications via email

When submitting a CV or job application by email, you must treat it just like a written approach with a cover letter included. You could put the content in the body of the email (no need to include postal address of yourself or the recipient) or you could have the letter as a second attachment. That way you maintain all formatting. In that case, the email can be short.

When attaching your CV do not call it *CV2011*, how will the recruiter find this again? Much better to name it something like *DSmithCV*, or even better, *DSmith_electrical_engineer*.

Review the email address you use. For work, use a more formal email address such as dk.smith@gmail.com. Also avoid emoticons, like ☺ (happy face) it does not create a business-orientated impression and may lead to your message being considered spam. Don't forget to create a signature line so that all job emails can go out with your contact details automatically included at the end of each mailing.

How to follow up

It can be tempting to call a company to check that your application was received. However this is just asking them to do some work (check their records) for no gain to them. To follow up effectively, make sure you demonstrate some of your strengths. Pick up the phone and have a conversation in which you can demonstrate something in addition to your application or something to emphasise. Perhaps you could relate something in the news relevant to the company or industry.

If you can't call, send an email. You could say something like

> *I am extremely interested in the high quality products and services offered by your company, and XXXXX is exactly the kind of company I want to work for. (Reemphasise some key points from the initial letter.)*
>
> *My CV was sent to you on 3 August 2011. I wish to emphasise my interest in the role of marketing manager.*
>
> *I look forward to talking with you soon and will call you on Thursday, ready to answer any questions you may have.*

By taking the time to follow up, you are demonstrating your interest in this job. If they tell you that you should hear within a further 5 or 10 days, make a note when to follow up.

Why you may not get shortlisted

Sometimes an application can be excellent but people still don't get shortlisted. This could be attributed to factors outside your control, such as

- The job is already filled but the company policy is such that they have to go through the motions of advertising.

- Some recruitment agencies place ads to get people on their books.

- Organisational changes may mean there is no longer a need for the job to be filled.

- Other candidates more closely match the employers' requirements.

- Or it could be that the company is so busy that recruitment is at the bottom of their priority list and even though they conducted the interviews, they have yet to get around to making a decision.

All of these reasons are outside your control, so don't blame your CV or cover letter when nothing you could have done would have made a difference.

Visit the website to download the additional resources:

- More examples of how to answer competency based questions on application forms.

Chapter Twelve

THE COVER LETTER

WHY YOU NEED A COVER LETTER

If your cover letter/email says *"here is my CV"* then it is of little value. However, a highly focused cover letter or email clearly makes a difference and it can be 50% of your marketing approach.

Most people send out letters, application forms and CVs with little attempt to match their skills and experience to the job requirements, and with just a very brief note; this is a missed opportunity. Others may send a detailed letter but it is long and waffly and not focused on the job. They will often include statements that sound grand but don't have specific examples to back them up:

- Vast knowledge – what kind of knowledge?
- Willing to go that extra mile – so what did he do?

The cover letter **must** focus on the needs of the company and refer to the detail you get from the job ad and further information. Following this structured approach below will give you the advantage over other applicants.

When you review a job ad you should check carefully how you meet the requirements of the job. This can then be used to structure a cover letter. You make it absolutely clear how you meet the requirements of the job, which makes it easy to be shortlisted.

Here is a typical ad for a retail supervisor in a large department store:

THE JOB AD

As a Supervisor you will report directly to a sales manager and will be responsible for the day-to-day running of a multi million pound turnover department and its sales team within the store which could include: Cosmetics, Accessories, Childrenswear, Menswear,

Womenswear and Home. You will drive the highest levels of **customer service** at all times and ensure excellent **product presentation** and availability.

SKILLS

You will be a positive, confident and proactive individual who has a **passion for selling and retail. Strong commercial skills** are preferable with the ability **to make effective decisions**. You will have **excellent communication, delegation and time management skills** as well as being a **proven leader** who can motivate and coach people to achieve. **Numeracy** and **computer literacy** skills are essential.

You can see how I've highlighted the key requirements of the job. The cover letter should then cover these points.

Take a structured approach such as using the layout below to match your requirements to the ad. You do this as part of your application preparation; it can also be used to create a cover letter. You could send the letter with a layout similar to this or choose one of the alternative layouts described later in this chapter.

Retail Supervisor

Key requirements	How I match up
Highest levels of customer service	
Excellent product presentation	
Passion for selling and retail	
Strong commercial skills	
Excellent communication	
etc	

You can them create a letter that matches the key requirements in the job ad and job description. I would expand further, based on what else was in the advert. Below you can read the letter that Peter sent following some coaching from me which resulted in an interview.

BRISTOL - SUPERVISOR - FT

JOB REF: MISSI0296778

I am very interested in the role of Supervisor, and believe I have the experience and many of the qualities to enable me to be successful in the role.

Key aspects of my background include:

Customer service: Demonstrated my ability to put the customer first, no matter what the current work priority might be. I offered to drop off products at local elderly residents' houses if they were unable to visit the store, and provided a community atmosphere where customers were actively invited for their input into product selection.

Product presentation: A naturally keen eye for presentation; ensured products and faced-up stock were replenished. Identified counter lines & products relating to current media attention in an easily accessible and identifiable presentation making full use of professional POS Material.

Passion for selling and retail: With seven years of retail experience, I love to serve customers and to offer great value and exceptional service, thus making a profit.

Strong commercial skills: Both practical and theoretical experience, including making use of professional commercial research & planograms. Clear understanding of all areas of the sales process & commercial awareness though experience at Stars News Limited.

Ability to make effective decisions: As manager of Stars News Limited, I made many decisions including the introduction of electronic payment processing & national lottery application. Decisions based on effective planning and implementation.

Excellent communication skills: Able to communicate with a diverse range of people. While volunteering with Victim Support I exercise care and sensitivity; in my work with Stars News Limited I am more commercial and sales focused.

Excellent delegation skills: Specific examples include communicating with part-time staff at Stars News and introducing a 'Notices Book'. When delegating tasks to staff, I always ensure that requirements have been fully understood and that staff are happy with what has been asked of them.

Excellent time management skills: Demonstrated my effective and successful time management between my responsibilities at university and my work at Stars News Limited. Also, throughout my university work, all my assignments and projects where handed in complete and to deadline.

Proven leader – motivation and coaching skills: I believe I possess natural leadership skills though working for Stars News Limited from the age of 16 with four years as manager. My style is non-autocratic, always seeking to take opportunities for input or change. I also took on project leadership roles at university.

Numeracy: My capabilities in numeracy are demonstrated though completing finance and economic modules at university and dealing with profit and loss and percentage margins within Stars News Ltd.

Computer literacy: I am an avid computer user with practical experience of Windows operating systems and Microsoft Office applications. My word-processing skills are excellent.

I trust you will find my details of interest and I look forward to hearing from you in due course.

Yours sincerely,
Peter Maine

TOP TIPS FOR YOUR COVER LETTER

Tailor your answer carefully to the keywords of the advertisement. Provide key examples of your achievements that relate to the key criteria of the position. Incorporate into your letter terminology the employer has used in the ad, written job description, or in a conversation. Don't forget to match THEIR NEEDS to YOUR EXPERIENCE and ABILITIES. Your letter should expand on your CV and complement your career summary, which you will adapt for each job you apply for. Find relevant achievements in your work history and quote one or two succinctly and colourfully. It's fine if you have also included them on your CV. Display good judgement by selecting the right, relevant information. Make sure the CV and letter are fully focused on the job.

Tailor your letter to a particular company; for example, a firm of solicitors or a computer games company. You will have researched the company as part of your preparation, so when explaining why you are interested in the organisation or position, avoid general statements like "*I am impressed with your products and growth.*" Write specifically about what products, what growth, and why you are impressed.

Consider using the same font and address style for both your CV and your cover letter for a consistent, professional look. Don't forget to put the job title at the top of the letter, and reference number where applicable. Avoid the phrase "*I am writing*" in your opening paragraph, as this is obvious. Address the letter to a specific person; if the advert doesn't mention one, ring the company and ask who to send the letter to. Make it clear that it was written for the addressee, and it is not a generalised letter. Lengthy paragraphs are overwhelming to read, so divide text into shorter chunks, when necessary, to keep paragraphs short. Pay attention to details. Type the letter and be sure to use a spell check. And read it carefully. Too many people send things out with errors in grammar, style, and punctuation.

If seeking to change sectors, compare common cultural links between the two work environments, such as the fast moving nature of retail with that of information technology. Answer the question of "*Why you?*" What makes you worth considering? Emphasise your positive assets such as education, experience, skills, accomplishments and personal qualities in relation to the employer's needs. You may be competing with recent graduates who will work for a much lower salary, so your letter has to emphasise your strengths and experience and how you will get things done much more quickly.

Too many I's

> *I am writing to apply for the vacancy of sales negotiator I saw advertised in the Gloucestershire Echo. I believe I would be a good candidate for this position as I have good interpersonal skills, and have experience of selling through work at both Vodafone and Boots the Chemist Ltd. I am pleased to include my CV for your consideration and I look forward to hearing from you.*

Above is an actual letter drafted by a client of mine. **The word 'I' is used 7 times.** The focus should be more on the company, so this letter needs to be rewritten. I've looked at how others do this, and too often it's just a case of changing the word 'I' to 'my.' But this still puts the emphasis on you. For example:

> *My 2 years of successful experience in online customer support with a web site processing 250 orders a day, my strong interpersonal skills, and my education fit the requirements of the website customer support opening you have posted on Career Builder.*

I rewrote this:

> *With high levels of customer support experience, gained through working in online customer support, I have the necessary skills for success in this role, including an ability to deal with difficult and challenging customers who have a problem, responding quickly to queries, and providing the customer with a calm and customer-orientated environment.*

You have already looked at Peter's cover letter which resulted in an interview. It's now time for you to have a go. Here's the structure for the letter; read it through and then create one. If you try and apply without a job in mind, it's hard to be specific enough, so if you don't have a job to apply for, base it on a previous application.

This is set out for a cover letter you will post. If you email you don't need to include the initial contact details.

A STRUCTURE FOR A COVER LETTER SENT BY POST

Your name
Your street address, postal town and post code
Your phone numbers, including mobile and your email address

Date

(Three line spaces between the date and the company address).

Name and job role of person you are writing to
Company name, Address 1, Town, Post code
Dear name of person

Opening paragraph: State why you are writing, identify the position for which you would like to be considered, and indicate how you heard of the position. (If you are sending a letter of interest which is not in response to a specific job opening, simply indicate the type of work you are seeking). Be specific. Also, make sure you sound interested and explain what interests you about the job. If you know someone who works for this company you can include a name check to them here.

Middle paragraph(s): Your goal here is to show how you can be useful to this particular organisation. Describe what strengths you have to offer this employer by showing the relationship between your skills and experience, and the vacancy. You can also describe your previous achievements and how they relate to the vacancy, and identify three reasons why you should be called for interview.

Refer the reader to your enclosed CV for additional information.

(You can divide this into a couple of smaller paragraphs rather than have one large, dense paragraph.)

Closing paragraph: End your letter by clarifying what will happen next and how they can most easily reach you.

> Yours sincerely,
>
> Space for your signature. If you are going to post the letter, use blue ink – it stands out!
>
> Type your name beneath your signature
>
> Enclosed: CV

Now review what you have produced. Are you happy with yours? Put it to one side and come back to it in an hour or so to look at it more objectively.

A worked-through example

Let's now work through an example of some work I did with Kim.

Step 1: Kim finds a suitable job

She contacted the employer for further information and this was all that was available (ideally you'll get more than this to work with):

THE JOB AD: TRAINEE CASE HANDLER

Job description

This role is based within the Recoveries and Finance team at our Manchester office and will involve being trained to manage your own caseload of recovery cases. Apart from the academic side, practical training will include learning how to open/close files, put on debts, archive and issue court proceedings.

Qualifications/experience

- Good communication skills
- Client management skills
- Team player

- Attention to detail
- Willing to learn academic part of the law/prepared to study
- Proactive
- Clerical experience

Possibly from an admin background or perhaps educated to degree level or equivalent would be helpful.

Step 2: Read the more detailed job description

Usually there will be a detailed job description and person spec. You will want to read this through carefully and highlight any key points you need to refer to in your application.

Step 3: Read through the ad and identify some areas to research further

Research will help you understand more about the company you are going to apply to and give you some pointers as to where and how to follow up. In this example, you will want to have at least glanced at the publications and be ready to ask an intelligent question at interview to demonstrate you have taken the time to find out more about the employer.

Step 4: Prepare the letter, making sure to address the key criteria

Your letter, along with your CV, is going to be used for shortlisting purposes. One way you can make things easy for the person doing this is to provide examples alongside key criteria.

Trainee Case Handle Reference No: HJ 987

Dear Miss Dixon:

I'm very interested in your advertisement for a Trainee Case Handler and have pleasure in enclosing my CV for your perusal. I have been working as a Legal Executive where I have developed many of the skills used by a Case Handler. I have detailed below how I meet your required qualifications and experience.

Communication Skills: I have excellent communication skills, dealing professionally with a diverse range of people including estate agents, mortgage brokers, bankers, surveyors and other solicitors. I enjoy building good working relationships and have developed a good rapport with clients who returned to instruct me on further matters.

Client Management Skills: Experienced in working in a professional manner for high profile clients who have recommended me to others. This has resulted in a number of letters of appreciation, available on request. My high level of commitment and integrity results in excellent client-care survey comments. I have represented the firm at corporate and client entertaining events. My commitment to an organisation is demonstrated by my willingness to work over and above the call of duty on behalf of my clients to achieve the desired goals.

Team Player: I have deputised for solicitors and partners in three different offices. I assisted locums especially during extremely busy periods when they were only employed part-time to cover my colleague's heavy caseload, and on one occasion the locum thanked me with a bouquet of flowers. I have demonstrated flexibility by cancelling my holiday to assist the team and enjoyed good relationships with all the support staff and other departments within the firm.

Proactive with Attention to Detail: Working on my own caseload, I confidently used my initiative to deal with a wide range of legal work including complicated matters in which I carried out research to answer enquiries. Working methodically, I proactively dealt with any problems that arose. I enjoy working under pressure and with tight deadlines and am able to prioritise my work according to internal and external influences using the case management system to diarise and monitor tasks and appointments. I also regularly review the priorities of my work to meet urgent demands

Clerical experience: I have experience of using both DPS and Eclipse case management systems and I am also currently studying the European Computer Driving Licence course, passing Module 2. Working as both a paralegal and a fee earner, I have experience of opening and closing files, as well as archiving and managing client accounts.

Due to the downturn in the housing market I have recently been made redundant and believe this is an exciting opportunity allowing me to use all my existing skills in a new area of law. I enjoy learning new skills and have proven ability to change career successfully.

I look forward to hearing from you.

Yours sincerely,

Kim sent the above letter with her revised CV and was shortlisted for the job.

Making an impact

Your CV is focused on past achievements; make sure your cover letter includes details on how you can help the organisation. What is it that you can include that will demonstrate what you can do to make a difference to this company?

SALARY QUESTIONS

An advert will sometimes ask about your salary requirements. You should never mention salary unless specifically asked. It may be too high or too low and provide the employer with an excuse to screen you out. Leave discussion on your salary and benefits package until much later in the selection process. However, sometimes a company wants you to be specific, in which case saying *"to be discussed at interview"* will annoy them, so it's better to give a range, such as 25k to 30k.

You may be considerably underpaid in your current or last job, and if, for example, you are earning 25k and the job you want has a salary range of 35k to 50k, you may be concerned that they will think you are not senior enough for the job.

Some people are looking to change career, and the jobs they seek may have a much lower salary. This may be because there is a need to take a 'step back' into a new career or for lifestyle reasons. Have a clear explanation ready.

Salary quotes can be based on many different things, and nowadays some companies will give you a choice of using some of your salary to pay for car, private healthcare, etc. So in addition to your basic salary, make sure you add on your bonuses, car, health insurance, gym membership, etc. Collect the monetary value of everything. Then you can truthfully quote your total package.

Chapter Thirteen

RECRUITMENT AGENCIES

What the agencies do

Recruitment agencies work on behalf of organisations to fill their vacancies. They are paid by the employer, sometimes for providing them with a shortlist of potential candidates, sometimes only for a successful candidate, so they are competing against other agencies.

They obtain candidates by coming to an agreement on a job description and employment specification, then advertise for the client under their own name. They may also approach people whose skills match a particular position and encourage them to apply.

These consultants are in business to place people and to satisfy their client-companies' recruitment needs. They earn their fee by supplying suitable candidates to their clients. To them, you are therefore a commodity. If they can make a profit out of you, they are interested. By understanding and accepting this, you will not have unrealistic expectations of them.

Making an approach

Dependent on your experience and background, you could approach local or national agencies. Lists of agencies and consultants can be found in Executive Grapevine, available from the county library and also through a variety of online sources such as www.askgrapevine.com/jobs/a-to-z/.

Firstly, spend time on planning and preparation. Treat it with as much care as an application. Choose the right agencies that deal with people with your background and experience, and demonstrate in your communication that you understand their needs and how you match up.

In a recession, recruitment agencies will be swamped with people wanting to get on their books despite a significant drop in vacancies. If you create a good relationship with an agency, you are more likely to be considered.

Too often people send out a generic email across a range of recruitment consultancies without any real understanding of their focus. If you want to work in finance in Bristol, why are you contacting an agency that places engineers in the South East? It demonstrates you haven't done your homework. Take care with your letters to consultants. They may not find you suitable for one position but could well have another likely to be on the market in the near future.

Make a call to introduce yourself and seek confirmation that they are interested in your skills and experience. They may prefer a one-page summary without your full CV and want to meet candidates before accepting them.

Don't expect them to be careers counsellors and tell you what you should be doing; you need to be clear on what you want to do, and why you are a great candidate for a particular type of work.

Remember they are working for the employer, and they are paying their fees. You are a commodity; if they can make money from you they will be in touch.

They ideally want to put forward someone who already does the job, such as for a competitor. If you have the transferable skills but have not done the specific job they are unlikely to shortlist you, so you must make it clear how you can do a particular job.

I've included a couple of letters which resulted in meetings with recruitment consultants. Read these through carefully so you can adapt ideas to create your own letter. You will see that they both contain specific detail to interest the consultant. Jack doesn't include his CV as this would dilute the power of the letter. Lance's letter is less detailed and his CV is attached. Either approach can work – keep track of which provides greater success for you.

Jack is an engineer looking for a new challenge:

Jack White
10 Elm Tree Close, West Town, South Shire WT41 9KL
07931 303366   jackwhite21@hotmail.com

Marie Williamson-Jones
Head of PFI/PPP & Major Projects, SSI Inc.

3 February 201x

Dear Ms. Williamson-Jones

As head of division in one of the foremost search and selection agencies, I seek your advice to ascertain what steps I may take in order to secure a move into a senior level of management within the PFI/PPP arena. I have listed below the areas of my achievements and experience which I consider are most relevant:

37 years of age and currently employed as Principal Engineer in one of the top 5 UK Engineering Consultancies, engineering qualifications to Degree level and a Chartered Engineer, Postgraduate Diploma in Business/Management and Administration (DBA).

My public and private commercial sector experience includes:

- Successfully managed operational budgets of £1.5 million per annum, including substantial human and financial operational resources within complex sites and environments.

- Commercial design and project management of construction engineering schemes up to £11 million, on time and to budget, in commercial/industrial/hospital environments.

- Initiated and implemented key management processes, i.e., QA systems, Intranet implementation and experience in the IT environment.

- Successfully initiated and implemented change management techniques, e.g., restructuring and integrating two engineering

- departments to achieve a flatter structure, reducing costs and introduce empowerment, and introducing process improvements utilising innovative modern maintenance management techniques.

- Well-developed communication skills, able to liaise effectively with client management, staff, contractors and consultants at all levels. Strong customer focus, results-driven and highly motivated with a proactive and pragmatic approach to developing and managing services and projects to optimise resources, reduce costs and improve customer service.

I will call your office within the next few days to discuss my experience in greater detail.

Yours truly,

Jack White

Example letter 2

Lance wants to gain another project management job:

Lance Lewis
6 Bodwyn Gardens, Cardiff, CF14 2PW
Tel: 07935 444567 E-mail: lewis@yahoo.com

Geraldine Moore
Thompson Butler Associates
Minister Chambers
Church Street
Southwell
Nottingham
NG25 0HD

Dear Ms. Moore,

RE: PROJECT MANAGEMENT OPPORTUNITIES

I would like to be considered for any suitable project management vacancies that you may currently be trying to fill on behalf of a client. Accordingly, I have attached a copy of my CV for your review.

For 16 years, I was involved in substantial project management for BT. This included most recently a successful £7 million project involving the move of 550 BT people with 'down-time' kept to an absolute minimum. I am also experienced in the facilities management of a number of diverse sites, including all aspects of security and safety.

I have been a successful team leader and have gained broad experience in contract negotiation, including tender adjudications for contracts up to £5 million. Apart from managing the overall facilities strategy for my unit, I was also responsible for arranging contractual rates for over 100 software contractors from agencies in both UK and India.

Throughout 16 years with BT, I worked successfully with managers at all levels and developed particular strength in the areas of both verbal and written communication. My role as project manager involved me constantly in problem solving to ensure projects were completed to agreed timescales, cost and quality targets.

I look forward to the possibility of discussing suitable opportunities with you and will call you on Thursday afternoon to take this forward.

Yours sincerely,

Lance Lewis

The reply

Most agencies and consultants will reply to your application in one of the following ways:

An immediate standard reply if they cannot use you. Your details will probably be kept on file for a few weeks or months and may be used to match against future assignments but don't count on this.

A phone call to arrange a meeting to discuss a vacancy. Often such a call will come in the evening.

For a specific job, a delaying letter will be sent stating that due to heavy response to their advertising, they are working through the replies. They could be considering your application but putting you 'on hold' to see what other candidates are like.

Follow up

You may think it preferable to follow up with a phone call but you may never get through. Even if the recruiter intends to call you back, their list of callers continues to grow. You may find it easier to send an email which can be responded to in a quiet moment.

Preparation for the phone call

If you contact an agency direct, prepare for your follow-up phone call to arrange the appointment. The information in *Chapter 17, The Phone and Skype Interview* will be helpful.

Meeting the recruitment consultant

When you meet with a recruitment consultant, you need to behave as if you are meeting a potential employer. Make sure you are honest, professional, well presented and polite. You must be familiar with your CV and be ready for a screening interview as they will want to get to know you and make sure you present well.

Recruiters have sales targets, and are targeted on making a number of calls and meetings a day, so don't be concerned if the call is short and any meeting lasts only about 10 minutes. Don't come across as needy; just provide the information they request.

If they ask you to format your CV in a particular way, do it! They may like to present all their candidates in a style that suits their clients. Some like short CVs, while others prefer more detailed ones.

You can ask specific questions such as:

- What is your business model – do you match candidates to jobs or jobs to candidates?

- How will we stay in touch (will they contact you or should you call them, and how often?)

- What is the current market like for {name of job you seek}?

- What advice can you give me to enhance my prospects?

- Do you pay travel expenses for interview?

As more than one agency may be in contact with a particular employer, ask the recruitment consultant to seek your permission before they submit your CV for a job. Otherwise, a potential employer could receive your details from several agencies which may dilute their interest in you. You can call the agency once a week to check on progress but no more or it seems like harassment.

HEAD HUNTERS

These companies are proactive in finding the top people within a particular peer group, often people who are not looking to make a change. Their contacts are such that if you are good they will find you!

Specialist executive search firms seek out suitable candidates for their clients. When a company seeks to make a new appointment they find candidates through both desk-based research and networking techniques. The research staff within these companies use advanced techniques to find people, including using Boolean techniques on specialist search engines. They look to find you even if you don't set out to be found. You might not appear in the search, but someone who knows you might.

They will identify relevant companies and key players within the industry; they will also seek candidates through a search online including LinkedIn.

This allows them to identify people who are currently employed and not actively looking for a job. They also talk with people they know to identify more potential leads. Their initial search includes looking for people online and you need to show up, hence the importance of being on LinkedIn.

Head hunters have a brief to 'go and find' a suitable candidate for a particular (senior) role. They do not keep a 'bank' of CVs and may not appreciate being bombarded with information. If you know a head hunter who has approached you in the past, it's worth a phone call to advise them of your availability and ask if they have anything that requires your background, skills and experience. It is unlikely that contacting a head hunter directly will prove fruitful, but if you do choose to use one, make sure she or he specialises in your specific area. You can find this out by checking Executive Grapevine at a business library.

Section 5
Active Job Search

Using CVs, cover letters and recruitment consultancies are passive ways to get a job. You need to be active, too, and do something different. Rather than wait to find a job, you can seek out opportunities. This is going beyond networking to being highly proactive. This section will show you how to make contact with companies, and introduce you to the many ways of getting found and to step ahead from those still using traditional methods.

Chapter Fourteen

THE DIRECT APPROACH: TARGETING THE HIDDEN JOB MARKET

In a recession, companies may be loath to advertise jobs. They know they will be swamped with applicants and leave the task for another time. Contact a company at the right time and you could be on a shortlist of one. The hidden job market consists of

- Jobs that will be advertised soon, but the details have yet to be finalised.

- Jobs intended to be filled internally.

- Problems that need a solution, and your showing up may lead to a job being created.

- Jobs that have not yet been scoped, so the job can be designed around you.

Taking this direct approach isn't easy. You have to do your research to be clear how your skills, qualities and abilities can be of value to a company, and you need the motivation to keep going.

> Many sources quote a statistic that 80% of jobs are never advertised. This is one of those myths! I've researched this and it comes from a reference to Sunday classifieds which only ever covered 20% of jobs. More up-to-date research by CareerXroads states that about 33% of jobs are filled internally, 28% come from referrals, 4.8% are from boomerangs (people returning from a previous company) and 3.3% from agencies. They summarise that 55% of new employees are from non-advertised sources.

When you take a direct approach, you will contact a company and highlight a few specific achievements that will make the reader want to meet with you. Most people are ineffective in this approach. They do minimal research and blast out a copy of their CV with a standard cover letter to every company they can think of, hoping there will be some interest. However, this sets them up for failure. Not only is this a waste of time, it can have a negative effect on your self-esteem. It's hard to stay upbeat when you are being rejected time and time again.

Undertake extensive research on yourself, the company and how you can solve their problems, and your success rate will increase. This direct approach works best when you have some very specific skills and experience to offer. If not, you may prefer to use the fact-finding interview approach. Depending on your background you can reach a success rate of about 4%. This means you need to send out a minimum of 25 letters to get one response.

THE BASICS

- Who are your target companies? Don't include only large companies; it can be much easier to contact decision makers in a smaller company.
- Within these companies, who has the power to offer you a job?
- Who can help you to connect with these people?

Step 1: Online research

You are clear on your strengths, skills, talents and experience. You now need to identify companies who are likely to have a need for these. You can identify companies via suggestions from friends, colleagues, and others in your network. You can also use press articles on companies that have achieved a take-over or achieved a new large contract. More guidance in *Chapter 10, Research for job search*.

Step 2: Phone research

Sending a letter, or message on LinkedIn, can set the scene, but don't let this stop you making the phone calls; nothing is as effective as talking with people.

After you have identified companies to approach, you need to find the right person to contact. This is the person you would expect to report to if you got the job. If you are more senior, a letter to the managing director may mean you are invited to attend for an informal chat to discuss possibilities that he or she is only just considering. Make a phone call to get the right name and job title, you can't rely on names that appear on the company website.

Step 3: Prepare your letters

In most cases, you cannot send out a standard letter to all companies; you need to personalise it to focus on your background and the specific company.

Think about the problems faced by the managing director, the senior researcher, etc., to whom you are writing. How can your combination of experience, training and aptitude help them? How can you make their life easier or more profitable? This is a time-consuming approach, but you will have a much higher success rate if you tailor your letter specifically, rather than choosing a mail-shot approach. Then send them a personal letter, highlighting anything that directly relates to contributions you can make, and include specific, relevant information. Do not be tempted to attach your CV as this will distract from your letter.

> You could make a cold call, or you could send a letter and follow up with a call. That's my preferred approach to set the scene and enable you to truthfully say to a 'gatekeeper' that the person is expecting your call.

Confirm you will be phoning later to enquire about a meeting, and make sure you follow up as you have promised. If the person is not available, leave a message to say you called. It's proof you kept your word. Arrange a good time and day to ring again.

Your letter may not only short-circuit middle management and HR, but it frequently makes it possible to get to see the managing director or another director of the firm.

It doesn't make any difference whether you are looking for a job that pays £10,000 or £100,000. Get that direct approach letter composed!

Client success stories

Paul researched alternatives to agricultural sales. His research led him to consider a career as a land surveyor because it would use his high level of mathematical abilities, as well as his degree and experience working in agricultural settings. He sent out 10 letters requesting an interview. The 10 letters prompted three meetings and one resulted in a job offer. It worked for Mark too. Mark had been working in a busy administrative office and was so busy that there was never time to think. He also had a difficult boss who would blame him for anything that went wrong. He was interested in becoming a legal executive so he sent out a number of such letters, was able to schedule a meeting, and was offered a job by the first company he approached.

Both Paul and Mark had relevant work experience, which meant they would have been credible candidates if they had applied for an advertised job. But their research, their access to important information, and their opportunity to talk with someone in their chosen fields allowed them to be considered outside of a normal recruitment process. They did not have to compete with applicants who found the job through advertisements.

If, like Mark, you are interested in becoming a legal executive with a firm within a 20-mile radius of your home, you can identify companies via an internet search or looking in the yellow pages. If you are interested in working in marketing, for example, you can find people by contacting companies and asking for the name and contact information of their marketing manager. It's a big plus if an acquaintance or colleague gives you an introduction, then the person you'll be talking with will already know something about you.

FIVE STEPS TO A SUCCESSFUL DIRECT APPROACH LETTER

Step 1 is to catch the reader's interest, to make them want to read the rest of your letter. For example:

> *As an assistant marketing manager for a leading consumer product, I helped increase sales by 13% through a new marketing policy.*

You should not start the paragraph with 'I.' You want to quickly show how you can benefit the organisation.

Step 2 is to make a connection between the first paragraph and its application to their business. It should relate to the company and their needs, not yours. For example:

Your company may have a need in your marketing operation for someone with my experience.

Your company may be in need of a sales consultant. If so, you may be interested in what I have achieved in sales.

If your company needs a manufacturing manager with my background and experience, you may be interested in some of the things I have done.

You can include details on how you heard about the company and why you are interested in working for them.

Step 3 is to give details of relevant achievements.

Include some of the bullets you produced for your CV and choose the most relevant for each particular company. Include a number of bullets to highlight your key achievements.

Ideally this paragraph includes a 'hook', something that demonstrates that you understand how you can solve a problem.

The fourth step is to mention your educational background including your qualifications, other education or training, etc.

The final step is to ask for, or suggest, some action or response. Give an indication of availability for interview. Be proactive by saying what you will do next, for example:

If you would like to discuss my experience in greater detail, I shall be glad to do so at a personal interview. I will phone you on Tuesday at 08.30.

OR

If you would like to discuss my experience in greater detail, I shall be glad to do so at a personal interview. I will contact Emma Joyce to see when you are available.

Note the ending; you are referring to their assistants name. If you were able to find this out, do include it, because it demonstrates you have done your research.

Don't be tempted to say, *"I would appreciate an opportunity to discuss any openings that you may have in your organisation."* First, *"I would appreciate"* suggests begging. Secondly, *"discuss any possible openings"* weakens your position. Remember that you are selling yourself in your speciality, not seeking general employment.

SAMPLE LETTER

Tom Prinder
1 New Road, East Town, South Shire ET1 0PP
07931 303366 tom@prinder.co.uk

25th July 2011
Mr. H. Mitchell
Finance Director
Pendleton Paper Products
Etc

Dear Mr. Bradley

Your company has expanded with great success during the last five years and is present in nearly every town centre. Perhaps your IT resources are sometimes overstretched, and in particular, there may be difficulties from time to time in establishing fool-proof systems at Point of Sale.

I am an IT Specialist with particular experience in the sourcing, development and installation of Point of Sale.

In addition, I have addressed the needs of providing effective training for all staff operating such systems, and ensuring that full online support is always available.

My last two assignments were with RETAILCO Ltd and BIZCO, who both needed effective Point of Sale IT equipment to retain customer advantage in the demanding retail food trade.

I attach my CV for your consideration, and would be happy to organise a time to discuss any aspects of my skills and experience in person. I'll call in the next couple of days to arrange a time for us to meet.

Yours sincerely

Tom Prinder

Tom's letter is a suggestion, but not a template. This is your marketing document and it has to stress your strengths and your benefit to the company. It should sound natural and be easy to read.

It is essential that the letter ends with what you want – to meet with a particular person. Make it easy for them to set up such a meeting with you by providing email and mobile phone numbers.

Studies by the British Direct Mail Association show that a catchy PS can increase response rate. What could you add? Perhaps something like:

P.S. I have written an article - 7secrets of effective point of sale marketing, let me know if you would like me to send on a copy.

Once complete, read it out loud to a friend or colleague and make sure they understand what you are trying to say. Check the phrases come easily; you don't want the sentences so long that you run out of breath.

Then put a reminder in your admin system to make sure you do as you have promised.

It can be hard to get started, so write an introductory paragraph; you can rewrite all or parts of it later if necessary. The purpose of the letter is to make the person reading it want to meet you and explore the ways you can benefit their company.

> The purpose of these letters is not to get you a job, but to get an interview.

Have you indicated you could solve some of their challenges such as increasing turnover, make savings to the bottom line, and developing new products?

Focus on the situation. Think about the problems that must be faced by the managing director, marketing manager, etc., to whom you are writing. How can your combination of experience, training and aptitude help them? How can you make their life easier or more profitable?

For example, if you are seeking a job as an accountant in a high-tech company, make sure all the information you give enhances either your experience as an accountant or your knowledge of the industry. If you are seeking work as a production manager, emphasise relevant examples. Don't dilute your message by including details of no interest to the one reading the letter.

Re-reading *Chapter 12, The Cover Letter* will be useful.

Step 4: Send out the letters

You could email but I recommend you post. A posted letter is more likely to be read; emails get deleted. A LinkedIn message could work, or send a fax. A fax is still taken directly to the recipient.

Use good quality paper; it does stand out from the emails printed on photocopy quality paper.

A direct approach letter should produce about four interviews for each hundred sent out. Remember, you must keep sending letters out. You can't just send out one set of 25 and expect to get a number of responses.

You should aim to send out around 20 letters a week. Keep sending them out even as you move into a second interview phase. Don't assume anything till you get an offer in writing.

As a rule, always specifically target companies and customize a letter for each. However, if you want to work as a trainee accountant, for example, you can send a similar letter to a number of companies. The example below, from Louise, was sent out to 104 accountancy firms. Her letter is structured around the key competencies identified for accountants.

> Aim to make 20 calls each week, and follow the lead from sales teams by counting down till you reach your target. Then celebrate!

This resulted in five meetings and one job offer. This letter is on the long side, but with careful formatting will still fit on one page. This letter was based on research that identified the key skill requirements of accountants.

> Dear
>
> Audit/Accounts Trainee
>
> Recent analysis of my future career direction, including tests and discussions with an Occupational Psychologist, has indicated that training to be an accountant is the right next step for me. The reasons I believe I will be successful are:

Business Understanding: Gained through a business studies degree and experience across a range of organisations such as XYZ Company. I have worked through periods of organisational change and so have first-hand experience of organisational challenges.

Motivation: I have already demonstrated this through the ability to work full time as well as study for a part-time degree. I set myself goals and do not give up.

Communication skills: I am used to producing reports and analysing data and have to explain complex issues to non-experts in an easy-to-understand way. My counselling qualification is evidence of my overall skills and I am noted for my ability to listen effectively to others.

Numerical skills: I enjoy using numerical data and am comfortable with interpreting figures.

Team skills: I am used to working effectively as a member of a team, and have contributed to effective teams in which we each had our own areas of responsibility and knowledge.

Analytical skills: Problem-solving is a key strength, I take a logical approach to analyzing issues.

IT skills: Proficient across the Microsoft Office suite and very comfortable with the Internet, and use of email and in-house packages.

In every organisation I have worked I have been praised for my high level of attention to detail and customer relation skills.

I appreciate that I am not a typical recent graduate, but believe I am a credible applicant due to my business degree and background, and the thought I have given to my future career direction.

I already have gained the following 4 ACCA papers (by exemption) 1.1, 1.2, 1.3 and 2.2.

I have had exposure within a finance environment totalling approximately nine months. This consisted of a placement within XYZ Credit Control department and a temporary assignment within Ambassador Financial Assurance.

I trust you find my details of interest and will telephone you in a few days to arrange a time to meet.

Yours sincerely

Louise Lawson (Enc: Curriculum Vitae)

In this particular example, enclosing a CV was a useful addition, but generally the letter is to encourage them to meet with you, and you wait to hand over your CV when you meet.

Step 5: Follow up with a phone call

Your aim is to speak to the recipient's secretary/assistant with the hope of scheduling a meeting.

Remember to:

- Call from a quiet location. Be pleasant. It may be a good idea to smile as you speak.

- Speak loudly and clearly.

- Do not use slang such as *uh-huh, right on, cool* etc.

- Listen carefully. If the person seems distracted, offer to call back at another time.

- Keep the call short.

- Have your letter in hand.

Find out to whom you are speaking and at what level, i.e., receptionist, secretary, someone who has just picked up the phone, etc. Don't let them put you off or try and put you through to HR. Be pleasant but clear on what you want.

I suggest you use a series of postcards, each covering a particular point. On the back of each, prepare how you will respond to objections.

Card 1: Introduction to the gatekeeper.

Card 2: Introduction to decision maker.

Card 3: Your reason for calling.

Card 4: Your main skills and achievements.

Card 5: A request for an interview.

Card 6: Close and confirm next steps.

Have a script if it helps you feel prepared and keeps you to the point. You can have the first question written out in full but make sure you don't sound as if you are reading a script. Use a large font for your notes and highlight key words.

A well-written script will

- Give you more confidence.

- Give a business-like structure to your message.

- Act as a prompt, not a crutch.

Don't expect a high number of people agreeing to meet with you. This is not a personal insult but a part of job searching and the nature of the recruitment process.

> Stay organised: keep a list of phone calls made, and outcomes such as sending on your CV, and note arrangements to phone back.

Getting past the gatekeeper

The person you speak to may be a receptionist, assistant, or private secretary who is skilled in the art of screening calls and diverting them from their hard-pressed boss. Part of their role is to stop you getting through. Be clear how you will deal with the gatekeeper. One useful technique is to find out the name of your target's assistant (you may have already done this to include their name in your letter). Learn from sales people and build a connection with this person. If you need help in this area, there are books such as *How to Start and Make a Conversation* by Christopher Gottschalk.

Don't tell the gatekeeper the purpose of your call, simply say you have written to (name of person) and are following up with a personal call. If he or she is unavailable, find out when it would be a good time to ring.

Once you are through to the relevant department, you should then say something along the following lines:

> *I wrote to Mr .... on .... You/he/ she should have received the letter yesterday, suggesting a meeting, and I am phoning to arrange a suitable time.*

If you are finding it difficult to get through, you could ring before or after work when the phone is usually switched to their direct line. Be ready to talk with them, because they may answer and you need to appear confident and professional.

Be ready to call back again and again. Don't leave your number, they are unlikely to call you back.

On the Call

- Speak more slowly and as clearly as you can. Vary the tone of your voice to add emphasis and variety.

- Listen hard and take notes; get them talking.

- Confirm any details before you hang up.

You can read more advice in *The Phone and Skype Interview*.

When you don't want to!

Too often our heads are filled with negative self talk. To help:

- Make easy calls first, so start with some calls to people you know.

- Don't waffle, get straight to the point and avoid starting with *"sorry to bother you"* or *"can you spare a few minutes?"*

- If you are calling because of a referral, mention the person's name.

- Have key points written down so you can refer to them. This can include having the opening sentence written out in full, using big print so you can easily see it.

- Think about possible objections and be ready to answer them.

- Wear a head set, it means you can relax more and it makes it easier to take notes.

- Be clear on what you want to achieve – if you want to meet, ask for a meeting.

- If the answer is no, remember this is just no for today.

GETTING A MEETING

Tom got three meetings out of 50 letters – a 6% success rate. There are a number of reasons people will agree to meet with you:

- The post has not yet been announced or passed on to a recruitment consultant to be filled.

- A vacancy has been announced, but your letter has interested the company and once they have seen you, you have successfully jumped the early part of the recruitment process.

- Either your skills interest the organisation because they are looking at new projects which require them, or your meetings have in turn led to the managing director looking at new projects requiring your particular abilities.

- The vacancy would have been filled by an internal candidate had you not written to the company at that time.

Step 6: At the Meeting

When you get to see the person, take a look at the meeting from their perspective. They will want to know what you can do for them, and why you wanted to meet with them. You must be prepared to think on your feet. Make it very clear how you can help the organisation.

You need to demonstrate your expertise and what you can do for a company. This is not a fact-finding interview but your chance to demonstrate your competence for the job or role you seek. Research will have identified problems, so dig deeper and get the person to understand how you can help. For example, if you are a communications specialist you could ask questions such as:

- *How many events will they exhibit at?*
- *What specific goals will they have?*
- *How do they measure success?*

The person you speak with should know the answers to these questions but often will not. You can talk about what you would do to ensure their costs are worthwhile, and how you can add value to the business.

Step 7: Follow up

Always send a thank you note to the person you have seen, and follow up as appropriate. For example, you could send a relevant and interesting article to keep your 'name in the frame' and to indicate your interest and initiative.

Chapter Fifteen

BEING FOUND, BEYOND LINKEDIN

The smart way to get a job is to be found. Recruiters are finding passive candidates (those not actively looking) through LinkedIn, and researching people through Google. To increase your chance of a positive connection you need to be clear about how you differ from candidates with similar experience, and ensure you can be found through having an online presence. You are far more likely to be Googled than found on a job board.

USING SOCIAL MEDIA IN JOB SEARCH

According to Jobvite.com, employers are using social media more and more to recruit new employees. Their research says that 89% of employers will use social media in 2011 to research potential job applicants so you need to be found. Having a LinkedIn account is not enough; you also need to be an active user of social media.

If someone googled you what would they find out? Positive examples, negative or nothing at all? Many companies will do a background check using Google and Yahoo, especially on graduate applicants but also on potential employees from all levels before the job offer. According to a survey of 102 executive recruiters by ExecuNet, an executive job search and networking organisation, 75% of recruiters use search engines to uncover information about candidates and 26% of applicants have been eliminated because of information they found on line (citing inappropriate comments, concerns about lifestyle and unsuitable photos and videos). According to *Search Engine Watch*, there are 25m to 50m proper name searches performed each day. So you must make sure only positive details are found when a company runs a search for your name.

GOOGLE YOURSELF

Have you ever googled yourself? If not, **do it now,** and see what comes up. Just enter your name into the search bar and look for the first four pages to see if there are any links to you. You may find links to your social networking sites or activities you have been a part of.

Now is the time to get rid of the non-business-orientated information. I searched for one candidate and found a page with him boasting about his excessive drinking. This page is from several years ago but still could result in his application hitting the reject pile. Remove anything that may stop you from getting a job, such as unfavourable articles, photos and comments. Also ask your friends to remove such information from their sites.

You may find you have a name shared by others. Several people are called Denise Taylor. One rides barrel horses, another is a researcher at university with a focus on wolf conservation, and another is a senior teaching fellow in clinical pharmacy. Searching for your name might bring up unsavory characters so make sure any potential employers are clear on who you really are.

You could have a common name such as Richard Lane; there are so many people online who share this name and I found a photographer, architect, scientist, solicitor and more. I couldn't find my client on page 1, so his presence does not exist – nothing good or bad is found. If he wants to increase his chance of getting found he may like to use his middle name or initial in all his online activity.

Do you have the right reputation?

Many people forget that information is available about them, as a private individual, online. Such information comes from our professional lives, our memberships in organisations, as copy of a conference talk, or through our involvement in committees, etc. But there is also personal information that we may not want accessed by people outside our circle of friends. These can include details from our social networking sites such as *Facebook, Myspace* and *Bebo* pages, or the photos uploaded on *Flickr,* and photos and comments that other people have put on their pages.

Ditch the digital dirt

If you have anything on the web that you wouldn't be happy about being on the front page of your local or national paper, you need to remove it.

If it is a page you have access to, remove the text or pictures. If there are items your friends have on their sites, ask them to remove them as well. If there are things you can't get removed, you are going to have to get things posted that will bump these lower down on the search engine page. Get started soon!

Can they really find my secrets?

What a recruiter may find is not details of sporting achievements and articles written for professional journals, but instead personal details you only want to share with friends. Comments made at 18 can later be found by a potential employer and can destroy the carefully crafted image created via CV, application form and interview. Not all companies will use social networking sites to search for details, but with so many doing it, shouldn't you make sure whatever you have written there or in forums is something you'd be happy for a potential recruiter to see?

The top three social media sites are

- LinkedIn with more than 100 million members

- Twitter with more than 200 million members

- Facebook with over 500 million active users and more than 50% logging on daily

Get started

Why not choose two to start with? With a focus on job search and career management, my personal preference would be LinkedIn and Twitter.

LINKEDIN

Chapter 6 talks you through how to get an effective LinkedIn profile so re-read this chapter now.

It really can be valuable to make contacts. Do be professional and build connections with people; it will be much more valuable than just seeking to add as many people as possible with no sense of developing a relationship.

LinkedIn is now taking over from job sites, as recruiters can search the profiles and find people who are actively searching, and also people they are interested in talking with.

Review your profile and make sure that it creates the right impression and is an interesting read. The first few lines are most important; too boring and bland and the recruiter may just quickly move on to another. Writing your summary in the first person makes you sound more approachable, and do include the keywords relevant for the sort of job you seek.

Your LinkedIn profile can be the equivalent of a first meeting, so don't be rejected at this point, just make sure you appear interesting and worth being followed up.

Also, think like a recruiter. If you were looking to fill a vacancy, what LinkedIn groups would you look at?

Don't forget to check that your LinkedIn profile and CV are aligned.

TWITTER

You can get an account set up quickly by following the advice on the site. Choose your full name as your 'handle'; you might need to add a middle initial if your name has already been taken.

Start by following some people, then begin to post short updates and retweet (forward) posts from others. You may well find yourself followed by spammers, so block these to stop them contacting you. Get a photo on this site, and a short bio, and link through to your LinkedIn profile.

USING TWITTER IN JOB SEARCH

- Follow thought leaders and key players within your desired industry. This helps you to understand the culture.

- Follow businesses you would like to work for, and post links to items that show your knowledge and interest in your areas of speciality.

- Allow 2 blocks of 10 minutes a day to review Twitter and find something each time to retweet or comment on.

- Build connections gradually; as you make more posts people will find you interesting and will want to follow you too.

- Twellow.com can help you to find people in your chosen field.

- Twitjobsearch.com can identify tweets about vacancies to match your desired job title and location.

- Monitter.com allows you to monitor key words of your choice.

- Twitscoop.com helps you keep track of trending topics.

FACEBOOK

If this is for family and friends set your security settings so no one else can see what you write. People will often add colleagues and their boss. You have to be cautious, since you can't brag about taking a sick day or moan about being hung over at work if your boss will read it. Monitor each time you are tagged in a photo. You can remove the tag from any photo you don't want to be associated with.

I prefer to keep FaceBook for friends, but you can still let your friends know about your job search, plus you can 'like' pages such as the companies you want to work for and sites such as facebook.com/amazingpeopleUK to get helpful advice and updates from companies that interest you.

If you are actively searching for a job, post it to your status update, someone you know might know someone who could use someone just like you and unless you share what you are looking for they will never know. You can also send a personalised message to all your facebook friends as part of your networking campaign.

Would you be happy for your mum to read it?

Whatever you type, make sure that you would be happy for your mum or a future employer to read it. Too many people have lost their jobs because of posts that should never have been made – bragging of pulling a sickie or tweeting that they are only in it for the money and hate the job. Companies use Google Alerts, TweetBeep and the like to capture any references to their company and will likely find out if you mention their name.

A teacher posted a comment *"By the way (class) 8G1 are just as bad as 8G2 LOL"*. Although this could only be seen by her friends, one of them was a fellow teacher who reported her, and following a disciplinary hearing she was sacked.

If you are likely to use social media as part of your job hunting, don't think you are safe even if your security settings are set to friends only – there are ways to access posts even if they are protected.

It takes time

You can't set up a profile on LinkedIn and expect to be offered a job, or send a general message and expect to get someone willing to talk with you. It takes time to build relationships, and that's why you must get your profile created and start networking online before you need help from others. If you are looking for a job, why not mention this in your updates. Let people know that you are looking for a job, remembering to make it clear what you want. Of course if you are currently working for a company you need to be cautious about what you say.

Have a consistent profile

If you have more than one social media account, and perhaps your own website or blog, then make sure you have a consistent description across them all. Make sure your CV, blog, personal web site or LinkedIn profile all show a consistent message with the same dates and the same photos etc.

PROFESSIONAL WEBSITES

As a chartered psychologist I'm a member of the British Psychological Society and am able to create an online profile. Most professional associations have similar facilities, so make sure you have a completed profile including a photo, and again, try to participate in any discussion forums.

CREATE A PORTFOLIO

You could create a folder of key examples of your work; have this ready to share with people you meet. This is a portfolio of your achievements. It can include articles, testimonials, certificates, and plans, all supported by charts, graphs and other visual images. Take it along when you meet people and use it to talk through your strengths. Create a master folder of everything that might be relevant and then reorder it for relevance before a meeting.

You can be found by creating an online version which you could share using Slide Share with a link from your LinkedIn profile.

A VISUAL CV

A typical CV is quite boring and static, but a visual CV is interactive and can be updated. You can publicise via your email signature and have links from LinkedIn, and every other place you communicate with others.

A visual CV is found online and this demonstrates that you are 'tech savvy'. It's the proof that you understand new technology. Ideally, you will buy the domain name which is *your* name. I was able to buy denisetaylor.co.uk but unable to buy the .com version. You may need to include a middle initial. This can then point to your website or blog. This does not have to be extensive but should contain a few pages with details of your bio, strengths, work experience, examples of your work etc.

A visual CV can include examples that move beyond your writing about your excellent presentational skills – you can link to a video hosted on YouTube or Vimeo. Create an audio so a potential employer can hear your passion for your subject.

THE VIDEO CV

Companies are now offering the service for you to have a video CV. You might like to review companies such as SupremeCV.com (there are many more and this is not a recommendation). My main concern about a video

CV is that it takes much longer for a recruiter to watch than the cursory 30-second scan given to a printed CV, but it could be useful once a shortlist has been created.

CREATE A PERSONAL WEBSITE

High-profile people such as musicians and actors can be found online, and in many cases you'll find access to information about them from official and unofficial sources.

Celebrities encourage this as it increases and enhances their media presence. You can do the same. Create a work-orientated personal web site to enable a potential employer to learn more about you. They are likely to Google you anyway, so make sure they will only read positive things about you. This can increase your chances of being hired.

A work-focused web site could include a number of pages to expand your CV. For example, you could include more detail on your skills and experience, along with copies of presentations you have made, pictures of you at work, any articles you have written, etc. You can also include non-work-related activities that could be useful, such as community involvement or independent travel.

A low-cost way to set up a website is to use a service such as weebly.com.

IMPROVE YOUR PRESENCE – CREATE A BLOG

A website could be based on blog technology, and many are now created using Word Press. You can set up a blog for free using *Blogger*, or at low cost using *Typepad*. You can have an 'About Me' page, a link to your CV and then pages or posts about your background.

Your blog could be integrated into a website or it could be a stand-alone. You must keep a blog current, so at least a couple of times a week you need to make a new entry such as comments on articles, daily news and your opinion on work-related topics. You could even document your job search.

A personal website, where you comment on current issues facing your industry, can introduce you as an expert on the subject. Blogs can be included in newsfeeds and can quickly get picked up. Someone I know who is a stress-management expert commented on the link between diet and stress, based on something she read in the paper, and found herself at the top of Google for that particular search term.

If you start a blog, you need to keep it up to date, and if it focuses on job hunting rather than raising your profile, be sure to clear it once you have a job. You don't want your new employer to think you are already looking for another job.

You can also turn blog posts into articles and upload on article hub sites such as Squidoo and hub pages. These can have links back to your website or blog.

COMMENT ON OTHER PEOPLE'S BLOGS

You can also comment on other people's blogs; this could create links back to your blog but will also get your name picked up by search engines.

ARTICLE WRITING

If you are quite eloquent, you could write an article that appears in a publication read by your target employer group. Many professional associations have journals and newsletters, and many companies have in-house magazines. To find out about publication details, contact the editor so you are clear on the typical length for such an article, how the article should be submitted, etc. You could also submit an article to an article hub such as ezinearticles.com. If you are going to submit articles, you can create a bio with brief details on your background. Base your bio on your marketing message and make sure to include a link to a website or your LinkedIn profile.

Writing an article can get you access to people who are otherwise unavailable. When making a cold call to ask about a job, it can be difficult to get through. However, phoning someone and saying,

"Hello! This is Jo Harvey and I'm writing an article on the challenges in charity marketing in a time of recession. May I please talk with your Chief Executive?"

stands a much better chance of success. This could then prove very helpful when you go for interview at a charity marketing department.

Once you have an article printed, arrange for reprints so you can enclose them with your CV or direct approach letters.

Client example:

Judy had a degree in interior design and was working as a waitress. She really wanted to get into journalism and was planning to take a post-grad qualification. To increase her chance of success I suggested she write a blog. I also suggested she write about areas of interest and newsworthy items such as fashion trends and reviews of restaurants and films to be included on her own blog or website and posted to other sites.

There are plenty of other ways you can comment, such as by answering questions on Yahoo, or responding to posts on discussions forums.

A well-designed and positive online presence can really help you in your job search. It really can make a difference – why not get started soon!

You could also create a special report based on some industry research that you could use both on your blog, and to send out. More details in the next chapter.

AMAZON BOOK REVIEW

As you seek a new job you can spend some of your free time reading relevant business books and write reviews on Amazon. This would be a good example of keeping up to date and is a great way to be thought of as knowledgeable. These reviews will also be picked up on search engines and will help to raise your profile.

Chapter Sixteen

TRY SOMETHING NEW

I love thinking about new techniques and remembering old approaches that will help my clients get a job, and I'm sharing them with you in this chapter.

Some suggestions can be seen as a bit extreme, but you may be able to adapt them to suit your particular situation. Many people have had success with radical approaches, and you may too.

Let's start with new things you definitely need to have:

MORE THAN ONE CV

You need your standard CV to be about two pages in length, but you may also benefit from three other types of CV:

- The Executive bio

- One-page marketing document

- Master CV containing details of every job you have ever had so you can use when required to fill in forms

THE EXECUTIVE BIO

The introduction could be a longer version of your personal commercial something that would still stand if it was read on its own, probably about 100-150 words in length. It is focused on your job objective.

This is followed by paragraphs on your key accomplishments, special skills, career history and education, and something that bit different! Within this, include some pertinent quotes from former employers, clients, customers etc. You want the person who receives this to be so impressed that they pick up the phone to call you.

I think these look best when kept to one side, stylishly designed with key information set out in paragraphs. Good use is made of white space.

THE ONE-PAGE MARKETING DOCUMENT

Yes, you have a CV, but will that be enough to grab the attention of your target audience? It's useful to have a one-page document that's a combination of a marketing document and a sales pitch. It focuses on key accomplishments and includes images, but most importantly it makes the sales pitch. This approach is not for everyone – it's for the fearless and the brave. Used more and more in the US, it's not so well known in the UK, but when done well it can make your job search rock!

- You do not send this to HR, but to a senior manager with the power to give you the job.

- You focus it 100% on the position you seek; nothing is generic, nothing is left to chance, and everything is there to make a point.

- You state brief teaser details, enticing them to pick up the phone and call you. You must have the facts to back up your claims once you meet.

- Use this when

  o   There is a high level of competition and you have to make a dramatic impact.

  o   You want to create a job when a vacancy doesn't exist.

  o   You want to change industries.

You still need a conventional CV as backup, but taking this approach will get you noticed.

MASTER CV

Your CV is likely to be a couple of pages in length and will be highly targeted to the specific job you seek. It helps to have an extended master

CV which contains full examples from every job. This is used to pull out the most relevant examples for the job you seek.

You may also like to consider:

FIND JOBS THROUGH THE BUSINESS PRESS

Find out about an expanding company through reading the business press. You can also see which companies are advertising, maybe not in your field, but if they are taking on employees in one area, there may be other opportunities soon. Job advertisements are a useful source of intelligence for your job search campaign.

CREATE A SPECIAL REPORT (WHITE PAPER)

A great way to be seen as an expert is to create a special report. This can be an analysis of your industry or sector and demonstrates your knowledge of this area. It can also enhance your credibility if you are looking to move into a new sector. Special Reports can be summaries of best practice or something topical. They can end with a call to action – the offer of further discussion or more information if requested. Of course, you will have links to all your online profiles.

To create your report you could contact key people working in the particular sector. For people who don't like cold-calling, this approach provides a purpose to the call. You are calling to seek information and you will be able to follow up with the person you spoke with when you send them a copy of your report.

Once created, you can include your special report on your CV and have it available as a download via your LinkedIn page. You can also use it to create an article or series of articles that are posted on article hub sites, and perhaps use this as the basis for a presentation that you include on Slide Share.

GIVE A TALK

You could create talks lasting 15 minutes, 30 minutes, or an hour on an area of expertise. Initially you could do these for free. Find out who to contact through searching for local organisations who often want speakers. You could also offer to talk to local colleges and universities.

You may be a recent graduate and think you don't yet have the expertise to share with others. However, your research will be current. If you have recently gained a degree in business studies or physics, people working in this field may be very interested in a review of recent research, or a summary of latest news. You could call every company that may be interested in hearing about this subject and offer to come in and give a talk, perhaps over a lunch.

ALTERNATIVES TO A PAPER CV

A CV does not have to be two sides of A4. You could turn it into a tri-fold leaflet, fold it so it fits inside a special occasion card and send this at Easter, Christmas etc.

If you are a designer you could create a booklet.

If your job involves analysis of numbers, think how best you can create a means of conveying this skill. If you think you are strategic, create a strategic report.

MAIL SHOT YOUR LOCAL COMMUNITY

Choose an area of about 50 houses or so. It won't take long to put a leaflet through each door with brief details of your skills and background and asking if anyone can help you gain work experience.

KNOCKING ON DOORS

With office-based jobs, it's less likely you can just turn up, but for manufacturing, retail and trade positions, and companies with high street offices, you could follow the steps below.

1. Print out 30 or more copies of your CV on high quality paper. Fold in half and put each in an A5 envelope.

2. Go and visit stores, and HR departments of larger stores and business units, to personally hand over your CV. Do this in the early part of the day when it's quiet. Avoid trying to make contact if the sales staff are busy with customers.

3. As you go into the store, have a quick look around so you can make meaningful comments.

4. Make sure to dress smartly to create a good impression.

5. Ask to speak to the manager. Tell them how interested you are in the store/industry. Refer to what you already know about the company and/or what you have noticed as you look around.

6. Hand over your CV.

7. Listen carefully to any cues they may give you. If they say they may be recruiting people in the future, ask if you should get back in touch with them in a couple of weeks.

8. This is a very important method and can't be done in just one day. It requires doing a blitz of different areas in your travel-to-work radius. This should be done several times a week. Many of my clients have got retail jobs this way.

Prepare a presentation

Prepare a 20-minute presentation which shows how you can contribute to the profitability of the company. Think about three problems the employer has and present a plan for how you would solve these. You don't need to go into too much detail, but you need to demonstrate that you understand the problems and know how to address them. Then directly contact a company to schedule a meeting to discuss.

Get to know the workers

If you are interested in working for a particular company and want to know more about them, you could eat lunch close to their building and ask the counter staff to indicate the staff who work for this firm. You would need to visit a few times, but you should be able to strike up a casual conversation eventually. In the meantime, sit nearby and you may hear some useful information; listen for what they complain about. Alternatively, you could go to a local bar on a Friday. After work, people often talk more with a drink or two, and in the conversation say something like *"If you could change anything at work, what would it be?"* You could then use the answer to create a targeted report or letter to the company.

Create a teaser campaign

Send out a series of postcards to the person you want to get an interview with. Just as in an advertising campaign, you give out snippets of information over a series of days, with the final one providing the answer: the need to call you!

RADICAL APPROACHES

Sandwich boards, Soapboxes, Billboards

These are both old and new, with origins in the hiring fairs of centuries past. It's about standing up and shouting out what you can do. It can include wearing a sandwich board, holding up a sign on the side of a road, or shouting out in the market square. You will probably get moved on but you may get picked up by the local paper or radio, thus publicising your cause. Don't let pride stand in your way. If you're up to it, such a display will also demonstrate self-confidence and, naturally, a willingness to stand out from the crowd.

In May 2011, Feilim Mac, a 'jobless paddy' spent €2,000 to get his message out on a giant billboard. This resulted in four job offers.

'Hire me' video or message

Take a different approach to a visual CV or website and create a teaser campaign to bring people to you. It could be the use of a QR code, buying a Google ad or creating a YouTube video or Twitter campaign that goes viral.

These will work by being unique to you, and will definitely give you 'the edge' if you want a creative job.

TARGET A WEBSITE AT YOUR IDEAL COMPANY

The previous chapter described how to set up an online CV/personal website. Matthew Epstein wants to work for Google in marketing and has created a website including a video targeted at this company. View his site here: http://googlepleasehire.me/. He was still looking when this book went to print.

Sell yourself on eBay

David Wood, an unemployed sales executive, tweeted about using social media to find a job, and with the help of a PR company created an ad to sell himself on eBay. His first ad was taken down for contravening eBay rules but the second one, selling himself as a product, got national media coverage and led to job offers.

Kyle Clarke wanted to get into recruitment and used Twitter to raise his profile. This lead to an eBay campaign – *EmployKyle* – that was picked up by The Guardian.

Create a FaceBook Ad

You could create a targeted ad, including a photo, which states the company you want to work for. Link the ad to an online version of your CV.

More extreme examples I've heard about include

- Hand delivering a box marked perishable containing a sandwich/ drink/ napkin etc along with a CV. The accompanying note says 'I know you are busy, but could you read my CV as you eat your lunch?'

- Sending a letter by priority mail such as UPS which notifies you once it has been signed for. You phone 15 minutes later to discuss your letter.

- Putting your CV under every car wiper in the car park near where you want to work. (I don't like the thought of all the litter caused by this.)

- Handing out leaflets outside a targeted company offering a free pizza to anyone who can get you a meeting with a particular person.

- Post an empty coffee cup containing your CV, a voucher for a free coffee, and a note requesting a meeting.

Section 6
Selection

The purpose of job search is to get to interview. You will have already undertaken extensive research to apply for the job. Once you get shortlisted you need to prepare for interview, psychometric tests and the assessment centre to perform at your very best on the day. This section is full of practical advice to help you.

Chapter Seventeen

THE PHONE AND SKYPE INTERVIEW

Many companies conduct phone interviews as the first stage of being shortlisted. This chapter guides you through the process of preparing to enable you to perform at your best in a phone interview.

THE PHONE INTERVIEW

The phone interview is used by executive search agencies, recruitment consultants and the HR departments of larger companies.

When I was involved in running large recruitment campaigns, we used phone interviews as a way of sifting through likely candidates to find those we definitely wanted to see. This left us with only the best possible candidates to interview. It also gave a good impression of our company, as people liked the fact we had a rigorous selection process.

We would phone the person in advance to schedule a time for the call. This meant that the interviewer could plan their schedule and the applicant had time to prepare. They were sent details of the job and the competencies being assessed, which helped their preparation.

Other companies take a different approach. Geoff was put on the spot by a recruiter who rang and expected him to be interview-ready without notice. I advise my clients to say it is not convenient, that they have to leave for an appointment in five minutes, but would be very happy to schedule a time for the interview. Following this advice keeps you in control and makes sure you will be in a 'peak state' for the phone interview.

Other clients have said that they have phoned for more information following seeing a job ad that appealed and then found themselves in a phone interview on the spot! You need to be prepared in case this happens to you.

> The main advantage of the phone interview is that you can readily refer to a lot of data. The main disadvantage is you cannot assess the body language of the interviewer.

Preparation

You should expect to get phone interviews so be prepared. Take time to prepare mentally so you sound energetic and upbeat. The call will probably come through to your mobile phone so have a professional message for when you are unable to pick up. Make sure your message is polite, direct, and businesslike and can be understood clearly.

> *"Hello, this is (phone number). I am sorry I'm not available to take your call right now. Please leave your name, phone number, a brief message, and the best time to reach you. I will get back to you as soon as possible."*

As you prepare for job applications, also prepare answers to probable questions.

When you talk you don't want to read out answers but you can have key points written down that you can easily refer to. If the call is scheduled, you can spread these papers out and have a pen and paper handy. Make sure you don't have too much as you don't want to spend your time looking for the right sheet of paper while someone is waiting for your response. You may like to have details on your skills, abilities and other strengths on separate index cards with examples on the reverse.

For a phone interview, keep in mind there could be background noise so have a quiet room to concentrate on the call so you can fully hear a question. Keep paper and pen handy for note taking.

Your voice is key, so be aware of how you sound. Record yourself talking and listen. Do you sound enthusiastic? Are you articulate? Do you speak clearly? Remember, the person on the other end of the phone won't pick up on your smiles and nods so you need to convey interest with carefully chosen words and appropriate voice inflections.

The call

As with other interviews, the outcome of a phone interview is often determined in the first few minutes.

- When you receive the call, stay on your feet. Most people project themselves much better over the phone when they are standing up. Try it with a friend or family member and see if they notice the difference.

- Background noise may irritate both you and the interviewer. Have a quiet room you can go to so that neither you nor the caller is going to be distracted.

- The call usually starts with confirming factual information and then asking more specific questions, often related to key competencies and characteristics of the job. In a screening call they are confirming the detail in your CV.

- Smiling can be heard in the voice. It also makes you feel more positive and self-confident.

- The phone artificially speeds up sound, so speak slightly slower than usual. The phone electronically depresses the sound of your voice, so put some variety into your speech.

Typical questions

The first question you may be asked is *"Is it ok if I record your responses?"* You will, of course, say yes! If it is being recorded, they may stop and check recording levels, so be patient.

You may be asked for a brief overview of your career.

Say exactly the same things you would say at a face-to-face interview. Prepare and practise this until it comes naturally to you.

Some recruitment consultants will use a short psychometric test, often giving you four options of characteristics from which you have to choose one which is most like you and one which is least like you. Don't try and second guess what they are looking for, just come across as a positive version of you.

You may be asked for specific examples against the competencies. These are the areas you would prepare for at a face-to-face interview, so get your preparation done ahead of time.

Finally, there may be general questions. These tend to fall into two specific categories:

Apparently difficult – such as *"Why does one need managers?"* They are really looking to see how you tackle a difficult question rather than searching for a specific answer.

Apparently easy – such as *"How do you spend your normal working day?"* This is trickier because they will be looking for specific content in terms of organisational ability and efficient time management.

Practice call

A practice phone interview with a friend or coach can help improve your confidence and technique. Often, when nervous, we waffle. You want to avoid this and be more logical in how you present your information. My clients are often quite nervous about this, so we do a couple of practice sessions, in which I first play the role of a kind and supportive employer, and then I am much more direct and matter of fact. We debrief after each call.

When receiving calls

- Be sure to sound positive and cheerful.

- If you are not ready for an unexpected call, say you will call them back (you have a dentist appointment perhaps?), and take time to get yourself in a positive frame of mind.

- Ask the name of the person who has called you before you start to discuss things, and write it down.

When returning calls

When leaving a voice mail for someone to return your telephone call, try to have the correct pronunciation of their name and make sure you state the following clearly:

- Your name
- Your phone number
- Your message
- The best time to reach you
- Your name again
- Your telephone number again

Then hang up gently.

SKYPE INTERVIEWS

Just a few years ago, video conferencing involved using expensive equipment, now it is much easier through the use of Skype. Maybe you already use Skype to talk with friends? It's free to download and all you need is a webcam and microphone.

Skype makes it easy to be interviewed for work when it would not be practical for you to travel. Yesterday I spoke with a company in Serbia to discuss running a training programme for them, and Chris was interviewed via Skype for a job in Dubai.

The benefits over a phone call are that you get the closeness of visual connection, see what someone looks like, and notice body language and facial expressions. A company can conduct first interviews via Skype and then just bring in the best two or three candidates for interview.

Get comfortable

If you have never used Skype before, set up a few video calls with friends or family. You see the other person and you can also see yourself on screen too (you can hide this so you are not distracted by it).

You can use the tools >> Options >> Video settings to ensure that you are clearly in shot. You can adjust the zoom and position, but don't set the zoom too high – you don't want your face to fill the screen; have some background as well.

It may be better to have your laptop on a stable surface rather than wobbling on your knees.

The background should be neutral; you don't want the interviewer to be distracted by the objects in your room.

Think about lighting – you want them to be able to see you, so close curtains if it is too sunny and have the lights on if the room is dark.

You should test the technology to make sure you are heard.

What's your Skype name?

Just as with your email address, make sure you have a professional Skype name.

The Skype Interview

- Make the video of your interviewer full-screen so that you are not distracted by anything else on your computer. Make sure to also be aware of any sounds or notifications that might pop up in the background.

- Turn off your mobile phone and ensure family and pets will not disturb you.

- Check how you look on the screen and make adjustments.

- Wear business clothes, and not just on your top half; you may need to stand up!

- Prepare to the same extent as you would for an in-person meeting.

- Have pen and paper ready so you can make notes.

- Look at the camera rather than the screen to help you make eye contact.

- Be cautious when having notes you refer to; each time you look at them you are not looking at the screen. You could have key points written on post-it notes on the side of your screen.

Chapter Eighteen

INTERVIEW PREPARATION

1. Introduction

Your CV can get you shortlisted, but you need to be able to perform well at interview to get the job.

There are different styles of interviewing and different approaches taken. Although you expect the person interviewing you to be a well-trained professional, be aware that many of those interviewing job applicants have little or no training. As you prepare for your interview, be ready for both.

Reading through books like this will help, but the best preparation is a practice interview, ideally with a skilled interviewer. You can still develop your skills by having a friend coach you through an interview, and by recording it so you can watch or listen to it again. Download an interview practice script from the website.

What is an interview?

Never forget the interview is a two-way process. It's not just the company wanting to be clear about whether you can do the job, what differentiates you from others, how long it will take you to master the job, if you'll display initiative, or fit in with other employees. It's a chance for you to make sure it's the right job for you and whether you would want to work for this company.

DIFFERENT TYPES OF INTERVIEWS

Screening

This is usually with a recruitment consultant and is often a short interview to establish whether your previous experience and competence appears to fit their requirements. You need to provide good, clear, factual answers.

Panel

This could be with two or three or as many as eight or ten people. It's used when a decision is taken by a large number of people and they all want to meet the candidates. There's less chance of bias but it can be hard to develop rapport. Answer the questioner and also look at others from time to time, noting any reactions. See if you can identify who holds the power and who may have the casting vote.

Formal one-to-one or two-to-one

You will probably sit opposite the interviewer(s) and little encouragement is provided. Be ready with specific examples – they are unlikely to help you out.

Informal

Don't be seduced by the comfy chairs and coffee table. The interviewer wants you to relax to encourage you to open up, so be vigilant.

> Some interviewers have no clear plan. They assess a prospective employee by means of a gut reaction and ask questions based on that. You need to be prepared for off-the-wall questions and learn how to anticipate upcoming questions so you can clearly make your points no matter how much a question might throw you off balance.

Second and third interviews

Some companies will expect you to take part in a number of interviews. At a subsequent interview, whilst the company will be interested in what you have done, there will be much more focus on what you can offer the company. You must show warmth, energy, commitment and competence. You will be expected to have a quick grasp of the issues and talk with confidence.

COMPETENCY-BASED INTERVIEWING

This type of interview is becoming more and more common, and you need to be prepared to give specific answers to specific questions. The interviewer is likely to have a set list of questions that will be asked of all candidates. Some interviewers will ask further questions if you haven't provided sufficient detail, but others will not give you the chance to respond a second time.

This style of interview puts less emphasis on first impressions and more weight on the specific examples you provide. Its format is based on the premise that the best guide to future behaviour is past behaviour.

The interviewer is likely to seek examples against problem solving, communication, motivation, interpersonal skills, adaptability, etc., so think through examples. Typical questions include:

- Can you recall a situation where you had to demonstrate your skills in problem solving? What was the problem and how did you tackle it?

- We all need to communicate clearly. Please give me an example when you have needed to do this.

- Please give me an example of when you have had to quickly build relationships with others.

Using the STAR approach in interviews

Most questions centre on your past or current attitudes, and your work, academic, or service experiences. When talking about these subjects, choose specific examples to illustrate your answers. Describe the Situation you were in, the Task you were asked to accomplish, the Actions you took and why, and the Results of your actions. This will help the interviewer follow your 'story' and see your accomplishments.

Here's an example of a response that uses this method to address an employer's question.

SITUATION: I didn't handle the transition to university well and failed my first year exams.

TASK: I knew that if I wanted to succeed, I had to develop better study habits and manage my time better.

ACTION: I created a calendar and marked the due dates for all of my assignments and tests. Then I set aside certain hours each day for studying, allowing more for exam times.

RESULT: My essays were in on time, and I took notes regularly to make things easier for exams. Because I was separating study time from social time, I would work hard and then relax, which has helped my time management.

INTERVIEW PREPARATION

General preparation

Start your preparation now. You don't need to wait until you get the interview. It helps to be well prepared as you could get a call for an interview at any time. And a call from a recruiter to 'come in for a chat' should prompt as careful preparation as a selection interview with the 'Ideal Company.'

There are four main areas of preparation:

1. Your response to *"Tell me about yourself"*.
2. Understanding your strengths.
3. Talking to your referees.
4. Researching the company, industry and interviewer.

You can then prepare for the main interview questions.

1: Your response to *"Tell me about yourself"*

The first cue is often *"Tell me a bit about yourself"* or *"Talk me through your career to date."* Too many candidates give a rambling life story, whereas a quick summary of key points is more appropriate.

You need to be able to provide a succinct and concise summary of you, your experience and achievements in less than a minute. Take time to make it clear, concise and interesting. Here's a common structure:

The 1-minute profile

Step 1:

You need to prepare an introductory sentence to get the listener used to the tone of your voice.

> *"As you are aware …"*
> *"Thanks for giving me the opportunity of an interview …"*

Step 2:

Provide a short summary of yourself and your achievements. This may differ depending on the particular job you are applying for.

Step 3:

This is where you provide a brief chronology of your previous employment, concentrating on achievements and skills gained. You should spend more time on your most recent career and your key achievements, and less on the past. Focus on the key aspects of the job you are applying for.

Step 4:

Conclude with a strong statement emphasising your abilities, and a question such as "Would you like me to elaborate on any part of this?" or "I'm a very creative and enthusiastic English graduate. What more would you like me to tell you?" Practice until it comes natural. On no account read from notes at interview.

2: Understanding your strengths

You must know the top five reasons why you will be a great candidate. Think of what you have achieved and re-read the achievement bullets you have on your CV.

Write out a question you could ask at interview which would allow you to use a particular achievement as an illustration. Do this for each of your achievements so you can use it to ask a question. For example,

> *"Is there a need to simplify processes? I'm asking because when I was in my last job I introduced processing mapping which resulted in savings of time and increased effectiveness."*

Review your career so you can highlight less obvious strengths that are relevant to this situation. You want to provide examples of why you will be perfect for the job. You are likely to be asked if you are well organised, so be prepared with a particular response such as how you switched 200 people from one hotel to another in 30 minutes.

3: Talk to your referees

You will need to supply references. If you were dismissed from your last job, check what your last employer will say if approached. You could negotiate an agreed statement. Many interviewees say one thing and their last employer another. Make sure what you both say is congruent. Don't forget to keep them updated on the jobs you are applying for.

4: Research the company, industry and interviewer

Too many candidates fail to research the company they are applying for, and the wider industry. See Chapter 10 for extensive guidance on this.

Problem interviewers

No matter how well you prepare, you may still meet with problem interviewers, so here are some suggestions on how to deal with such an interviewer:

The interviewer asks only closed questions

Closed questions demand a yes or no answer. For example, *"Do you have experience with Excel?"* You could answer yes or no but it's better to provide more detail. If the answer is no, you could follow up with how you are quick to learn or describe something similar that you have learned.

The interviewer monopolises the interview

Try not to encourage the interviewer by your non-verbal language or supportive comments. When the interviewer draws breath, you might say firmly, *"I'd like to respond to what you've been saying"* and keep going. You could tactfully ignore the cues that the interviewer wants to speak again.

You are faced with a very inexperienced interviewer

If the interviewer has no plan, use your own preparation to help the person out. If questions seem unclear or complex, try to handle the points one at a time. Sometimes you can answer one question while suggesting another one at the same time. For example, *"Yes, I made considerable savings at XYZ CO and that paved the way for my remarkable turnaround at ABC plc."*

If the interviewer runs out of questions, keep the dialogue going by introducing new material. Two useful responses for this are *"When talking about my experience at... was it clear that..."* and *"When I was describing what I did at... I should have added..."*

Another way to help out a nervous or muddled interviewer is to think what an ideal candidate would say to an anxious interviewer. This can help you to reframe the situation, focusing on what is important – the job, the criteria, responsibilities, etc. Referring the person to your CV can also help recapture relevance and direction. At the end of the day, you will want to reassure the interviewer that you are the frontrunner for the job.

GETTING READY TO ANSWER QUESTIONS

Interview questions are likely to cover your work experience, training, education and you as an individual to determine how closely you match the specification and whether you will fit into the organisational culture. You may also be asked about your outside interests and present circumstances.

If you want the job, you will want to prepare yourself so you can solve the interviewer's problem – finding the right person for the job. You need to concentrate on meeting their expectations, overcoming their objections, and demonstrating that you have the attributes, skills, experience and characteristics they seek. Make sure you can explain any gaps in your CV or answer any questions about the information it contains.

Although you can't predict what questions you will be asked, certain questions come up quite frequently. These are listed below, with guidance on how to answer them.

QUESTIONS

Tell me about yourself.

We covered this earlier in this chapter.

Why have you applied for this job? or Why do you want to work here?

An employer wants you to show enthusiasm and conviction for this particular job. You need to explain how well you match up. Emphasise what you can contribute, rather than how the job will benefit you.

Your response will be based on what you have learned about the company, so show that you have done your research. Explain what you have found and why it interests you. A really strong answer could be:

> "Based on the research I've done, <<name of company>> is a market leader. I was very impressed by the information I read on the web site about how you have gained a large contract and how employees are doing voluntary work with a local school. I like the way that the company gives something back. I was also impressed by the history of the company and how people work together on voluntary activities. This is exactly the sort of company I've been looking for – one that seeks highly motivated people who are keen to work well with others and help the company become even more successful."

What do you know about us?

Go beyond the obvious that anyone can find out from looking on the company website, to items that demonstrate you put in the effort to really understand about them. Re-read Chapter 10 to help you.

The interviewer could also ask you specific questions about the company, its products or competitors. Your research will make it easy for you to answer. In advance, think through why you want the job and what you can offer the company. This makes you much stronger at interview as you are talking from the heart rather than just giving the interviewer what you think they want to hear.

Why do you want to be a... mechanical engineer/chemist/store assistant/ manager, etc?

Every profession has a unique element so you should tailor your response to what is key about a role. As an example, for a nurse it could be helping people; for sales it could be competition and financial reward.

What are your strengths?

Tailor your answer to the interviewer's ideal candidate. For example, if you are applying for a sales position, you might describe one of your strengths (if it's true) as *"I've made a study of personality types and learned to quickly classify people in terms of the kinds of approaches that will most likely secure a sale."* Be prepared, in this case, to back up your claim if the interviewer suddenly asks, *"How would you classify me?"*

You might like to present your strengths modestly with phrases such as, *"At my last appraisal my manager commented that..."* or *"I was asking a client for some feedback the other day and they were kind enough to say..."*

What is your biggest weakness?

This question can sometimes be asked as *"How would your colleagues answer if we asked them about your faults?"* They want to see how self-aware you are. Describe a weakness which is irrelevant to the job, or how you are working to overcome one. I used to offer

> *"As a psychologist I knew my business knowledge was weak, so I took a business management qualification to bridge the gap."*

You could turn a negative into a positive:

> *"My biggest weakness is that sometimes I work too hard, and my life can get out of balance."*

> *"My colleagues have told me that I can be too focused on my work and I have to remind myself to lighten up."*

Be ready to expand on how this weakness impacts on your job. If it doesn't, they may well ask for another example.

You can also present your weaknesses positively. For example, *"I can get impatient with people who put up obstacles so I've learned to listen more carefully. I've found they often have a valid point, but they just haven't expressed it well."* It's often better to provide an example from the past so that you describe the weakness (such as finding it difficult to delegate in a first management role) and then how you overcame it.

> If you say that your weakness is that you are a perfectionist, an interviewer could ask if this means that you miss your deadlines or irritate colleagues. Say no and they may deduce that this is not a weakness and ask for another example.

What would your last boss say were the areas you needed to improve?

This is a variation on your having to identify your development needs. You could talk about one or two and what you have done about them. For example, *"My boss identified my lack of broader business knowledge, so I have started to study for a management diploma and to shadow people in other parts of the organisation."*

Why should I hire you over the other people I have interviewed?

The interviewer expects you to be confident in answering this question so be assertive and proud of your efforts. Say something like:

> *"With my four years' experience in the financial sector and a track record of simplifying processes and thus saving time and money, I believe I would be a great addition to your team."*

"I chose marketing because I enjoy working with others and I am motivated by success. Marketing allows me to capitalise on my unique blend of creativity, hard work and ability to learn."

This gives insight into how a person thinks. They want you to show you have put thought into this decision and looked into the future.

Be able to answer questions about your education such as:

Why did you choose your degree subject? (Often asked of a recent graduate)

You do not want to say it was because it was the only degree offered to you via clearing, or that your parents thought it was a good idea. Give particular reasons, and do so confidently.

What are your interests?

Make sure your interests are in line with the job. It's best to think in advance and have a balance of team and individual pursuits, perhaps showing leadership in a voluntary organisation if you are seeking your first management/supervisory role.

What are your short and long-term goals?

This should be in line with the job you are applying for. If you want to be a solicitor, a job as a legal executive is a step along the way. But if you want to be a doctor, why are you applying for a job as a sales executive? You could say:

"My short term goal is to join a company where I will be challenged and have room to grow. One of my longer-term goals is to grow with the company and move into management."

The person who is interviewing you expects you to want to stay with this company so don't give any indication that this job is a stop gap as you head towards what you really want to do.

Can you give me an example of team work and leadership?

Give an example of working effectively in a team, and also of a time when you took the lead. But don't let people think that you can only work with others. Give an example of working effectively alone as well.

Do you prefer working on your own or in a team?

If you know this is a team or individual job you can base your answer on that. It's probably best not to show a preference but to say that you enjoy both.

What was your greatest challenge and how did you overcome it?

Have an example ready which moved you outside your normal comfort zone or into a new area, but keep it focused on the job!

Why are you looking to leave your current job? Or why are you contemplating leaving your company?

You must have a reason. These could include that you are at a stage in your career where you want a job that is more challenging and rewarding or the company is at risk of closing down. Never be critical about your current company nor say your decision to leave is due to difficult people. They may wonder what it is about *you* that is difficult.

In a recession, companies expect some of their applicants to be unemployed, but you can make this sound a bit more upbeat, such as, *"I managed to survive two rounds of redundancy, but by the third round, an additional 20% of people were let go, including me."*

What major problems did you encounter in your last job?

Whatever you say, make sure the problem was overcome.

You don't have any experience of marketing, do you?

If it were a problem you wouldn't have been shortlisted, so don't say *"No, I don't."* Instead, talk about how you want to broaden your experience, how you are adaptable and quick to learn, etc.

Why did you stay so long with one company?

They were a good company and you were continuing to develop yourself.

You seem to have done a lot of job-hopping. Why?

You had to move to other companies to progress your career but you would much prefer to develop it in one company.

If you could choose any job what would it be? or What is your ideal job?

Do not start discussing your fantasies. The job you have always wanted is the one you have applied for.

What would you describe as your greatest achievement?

Be prepared to give an achievement that is relevant to the job you are applying for.

Are you ambitious?

You don't want to be content to stand still, but you don't want to be seen as climbing over everyone to get to the top. You could say that you are ambitious to do well, but job satisfaction is key.

Are you applying for other jobs?

Let them know you are in discussions with other companies. They will be reassured that others are interested in you.

What was the main weakness of your last boss?

Do not be tempted to say anything detrimental. People expect loyalty. Your reply could be

> *"I have the highest respect for my manager. He has supported and challenged me so I am now in a position to apply for a greater challenge."*

Would you be prepared to relocate?

You need to have thought this through in advance so you can answer honestly.

How would you describe your management style?

If you are a manager or supervisor, this should be easy for you. Think this area through in advance of the interview.

How do you prioritise when you are given too many tasks to accomplish?

This question is asking about the way you plan your time. Whilst you want to be seen as someone who is flexible, you will also want to show how you will manage your time by differentiating between tasks that are urgent and tasks that can wait.

Give me an example of when your work has been criticised. How did you respond?

Make sure you describe an idea that was criticised, not your work. A possible answer is that you suggested a new approach to your boss who told you exactly what was wrong with the idea. You listened carefully and realised he had some valid points. You went away, reviewed your work and came back with a revised suggestion which was better received.

What do you see as your greatest strengths as an employee? What have been your best achievements?

You already know your strengths, so refer to those, making sure they link in with what the new employer will want.

What would be the area you feel least confident about if we offered you a job?

You are being tested on your self-confidence. Expand on your strengths and what you can bring to the company and how you are looking forward to this new role.

How would your last boss describe you?

This is another question to allow you to describe your strengths. So think of something specific such as *"My boss told me I was a great team player, willing to get involved and someone the team could rely on."*

How would you describe your health? How many days sick leave have you had in the last two years?

Do not be tempted to lie, they can check this with your last employer. If it has been due to a serious illness, explain how you are now fully recovered and have not had a day off sick since xxx.

Would you accept this job if I offered it to you?

Of course! Answer yes without hesitation. You can save the negotiations for later.

Are you considering other jobs at this time?

Just say yes, and leave it at that.

How does this opportunity compare?

From what you've heard so far, it compares favourably and you'd like to know more.

What other companies are you looking at?

Don't mention names, explain the need for confidentiality in this area.

Where do you see yourself in five years' time?

The company wants to know that you plan to stay for a while, so stress your strengths and how you can use them in this job. Express that as long as you can develop and grow, you see yourself staying for quite some time.

Aren't you over-qualified for this position?

Tell them you see lots of challenges in this opportunity and that you will find the work interesting. Remind them of why you have applied for the job.

A PRACTICE INTERVIEW

You will probably be asked some of these questions but also be ready for some quite esoteric questions! I continue to be amazed at some of the questions my clients have been asked. Weird questions include *"If you were an animal, what sort would you be?"* What are they after and how should you respond? A panda might be considered too soft, a lion too aggressive, a snake... I think I'd like to be a cheetah!

Are there any questions you are afraid of being asked? You need to write these down and practise them!

Practice answering questions out loud will help.

To make it easy, visit the website and download the practice interview handout. You can then hand this over to someone who takes on the role of interviewer. Ideally, record it so you can play it back. Most people don't like to listen to or watch themselves, but it does enable us to pick up on any annoying habits.

Rehearse but don't memorise

Rehearsing before an interview helps. Think ahead, anticipate the questions and prepare answers, then say them out loud and time yourself. Never talk for more than two minutes straight and don't try to memorise answers word for word. You may come across as stiff and unable to function off the cuff. To help remember the answers, you could use a few keywords as mnemonics.

HANDLING THE SALARY QUESTION

We have already looked at how to respond to this in your application, but it can also come up at interview. Let's look at some of the questions you could be asked:

What salary are you seeking?

You want to keep this vague so you can move into the negotiation phase when you are offered the job. However, part of your initial research should be to understand the typical range for the job you are applying for. Summarise the requirements of the position as you understand them and then ask the interviewer for the normal salary range for that type of position in his/her company.

If they suggest a salary that is less than you hoped for, you need to be realistic with your options. Weigh up a drop in salary with having a regular income. It may be best to say that you would be very willing to discuss this once they are sure that you are the best person for the job.

What are your salary expectations?

You can ask what the normal salary range for this position is (assuming you haven't already uncovered this information). If asked again, distinguish yourself from the masses by stating, *"I am much more interested in doing (type of work) for (organisation's name) than I am in the size of the initial offer."* If asked yet again, a final response can be *"I will consider any reasonable offer."*

How much are you earning in your current position?

This is usually asked to cap your salary ambitions. Ask to learn more about the position before you get into detailed salary discussions. If asked a second time, have ready your research into the salary of the offered position and similar positions. If your current position doesn't provide a meaningful comparison or is comparatively low, then briefly spell out the reasons why this figure should not guide current discussions. You may be seeking out a career on a lower salary due to a change of career path or for a better life/work balance, but be ready to be able to explain the reasons why a lower salary is acceptable.

How much did you earn in your last job?

Tell the interviewer that you would prefer learning more about the current position before you discuss compensation, and that you are confident you will be able to reach a mutual agreement about salary.

"The salary range for this position is £22,000 to £27,000. Is that what you were expecting?"

Tell the interviewer that it does come near to what you were expecting, and then offer a range which places the top of the employer's range into the bottom of your range (i.e., *"I was thinking in terms of £27,000 to £32,000"*). Remember to be sure that the range you suggest is consistent with what you learned about the market rate for that position.

The salary is £2000 per month.

Try not to look excited or disappointed. Simply repeat the salary, look up as though you were thinking about it, and pause. Don't worry about the silence. Give the employer an opportunity to increase the offer. If the interviewer does not change the offer, try the response suggested above.

OVER TO YOU … QUESTIONS TO ASK AT THE END OF THE INTERVIEW

At the end of the interview, you will be asked if you have any questions. So many of the people I interview mumble about everything having been covered. It makes for a weak ending. The best candidates open their briefcase and pull out a pad with a few questions listed and choose three or four to ask, such as:

Since the job was advertised, have your requirements been amended?

This is a good question to help you to sell yourself by solving some of their newly defined problems. You can then send a follow-up letter addressing these problems.

What would you see as my priorities in this job?

This helps you to find out if there are any major problems. You may also find out there is a specific task that you can do easily, and give examples from your past.

How does this job contribute to the success, efficiency and profitability of the organisation?

An excellent question, showing strategic thought. In some jobs though, the interviewer may not know the answer, so beware of appearing too smart!

If I were to be offered the job, what preparation could I do?

This demonstrates your enthusiasm and interest, and it helps them to visualise you in the role.

I am very interested in this job and believe I can do it well; do you have any concerns about me as a candidate?

The interviewer may not like to commit themselves, but if they do, offer reassurance. If they were to say, *"We were looking for someone with more knowledge in a particular area,"* you can emphasise how quick you are to pick up new knowledge.

Imagine that I excel in this position. Is there room for progression?

Better to ask now then to find out later there are no real prospects. But things can change. Years ago, when I applied for a job as a Post Office counter clerk, I was told there would be no opportunities for promotion, but a move to a regional centre resulted, in less than a year, in getting a junior management position.

If I were to join the company, where might you see me in 3–5 years' time?

They are likely to have asked you where you see yourself, so find out if they see the job as part of a career path. You can follow this up as appropriate.

Before leaving today, would I be able to look around?

It shows enthusiasm and even if they say no, nothing has been lost.

I'm really impressed with your company, its products/services and everyone that I have had the opportunity to meet. I'm confident I could do a great job in the position we've discussed. When can I expect to hear back from you?

Try to get a specific time after which you can follow up if you haven't heard anything.

A perfect close

Make sure you deliver a one-minute closing statement.

It must be short and to the point and 60 seconds is the absolute maximum. You must know the top five reasons why you will be a great candidate, and be able to weave these into the discussion. This is your chance to summarise your qualifications for the position, your top skills, experience, and accomplishments so the interviewer is really clear on why they should hire you.

Thank the interviewer, and be sure to ask about the next step or stage. Failure to do this may leave them in some doubt as to whether you wish to proceed.

If you realise that the job isn't a great fit, make sure you still leave a good impression. You may be considered for another vacancy.

Visit the website to download the additional resources:

- Further examples of competency based questions
- Mock interview handout

Chapter Nineteen

THE INTERVIEW - YOU'RE SHORTLISTED!

Introduction

When you get the letter asking you to attend an interview, it should tell you:

- The nature of the interview
- Whether there will be any psychometric tests
- Who will interview you, with name and position
- If you will be given a tour of the company
- Who you will meet

Ring to confirm the interview place, time, day and date. This is another opportunity to record a good impression. Request the job description if one has not yet been sent. If you have any special needs or disabilities, forewarn the company.

Your Preparation

You completed extensive research when you made your application; it's time to re-read this and to identify further helpful information. The research chapter will be helpful. Think carefully of your strengths and the requirements of the job, and the questions the interviewer may ask. Many will ask questions based on your application form and CV so be ready with full answers and clear examples.

Be clear on your work history and other experience that will enable you to demonstrate your ability to do the job. You may look good on paper but can you back it up when they meet with you?

> You will gain a competitive edge if you can demonstrate your knowledge of the industry you are applying to, not just knowledge of the role you have applied for.

Your preparation should go beyond what the other candidates will do. Of course you will have looked at the company website, but be sure to have a view on the competitors and industry developments, and know what is happening right now through a news search in the business press and from comments on public sites.

Key guidance for the interview

Preparation – final check. I need to…

- Carefully match my background against the job description and person spec. Re-read the job advertisement and review my CV and career history to be ready to answer questions and go into more detail on any topic.

- Find out the names and position(s) of the interviewer(s), research the company and the person/people who will be interviewing, as well as current and future business issues.

- Practice interview questions and prepare questions to ask (it's fine to have them written down).

- Produce a concise statement to explain why your previous employment ended or why you want to leave.

- Drive to the interview location in advance so you know where it is and where you can park.

- Plan what to wear. Make sure your clothes are clean and you feel comfortable wearing them.

  AND check for any breaking news that might impact on the company.

DON'T GET TOO EXCITED ABOUT A FORTHCOMING INTERVIEW

Don't start dreaming that you already have the job and stop your job search. Keep looking as hard as ever until you get the contract. When you get an interview always have another one lined up, including a fact-finding interview, so it will stop you coming across as desperate.

On the day

- Have something to eat beforehand. Sometimes interviews are delayed and you may find that there has been no opportunity even to obtain a snack.

- Dress professionally, clean and neat.

- Make sure you know where to go and how you are going to get there.

- Allow extra time for the journey going wrong.

- If you chew gum, remove it before you get out of the car.

- Take a mint to freshen your breath.

- Be confident and expect to do well.

- If you know your hands can get clammy, use antiperspirant spray.

- Aim to arrive with time to spare, so that you can be as relaxed as possible.

What to take

- A briefcase or folder. In this you can keep:
    o Copies of all correspondence received.
    o Spare copies of your CV.
    o Notebook with your questions listed.
    o A good quality pen.
    o Something to read in case you are kept waiting.

Also, wear a watch so you know the time.

The journey to interview

The importance of being on time to the interview cannot be overstated! It is crucial for you to find out its exact location. If possible, drive to the location a day or so before at the time you will drive there on the day of the interview. This way, you can adequately estimate how long it will take. Ask yourself if you can get to the building via another route, and allow for any obstruction that could occur along the way (such as road construction, traffic, or public events).

WHEN YOU ARRIVE:

- **Be punctual.** Don't just be on time, be ten minutes early. Use this time to re-check your grooming and comb your hair.

- **Be appropriately dressed.** Dress as you would on the job. The interviewer does not expect a welder in a three-piece suit or a sales manager in jeans.

- **Switch off your mobile phone**. You don't want to have the embarrassment of it going off when you are with the interviewer.

- **Be friendly but not over-familiar.** When speaking with receptionists and administrators, remember that they may later be asked by the interviewers to comment informally on the way candidates have conducted themselves outside the interview proper.

- **Visit the toilet.** Not just for natural reasons but walking to and from the toilet will often take you past working areas of the office from which you can indirectly glean a great deal of information about a company, e.g., cleanliness, atmosphere, friendliness, efficiency, etc. While you are there, check how you look. Is your tie straight? Shirt tucked in? Nothing stuck in your teeth? I've lost count of the people I have interviewed with windswept hair and a wayward tie.

- **Be prepared to shake hands.** Make sure your hands are dry. A firm handshake reflects your confidence level. Your handshake should never be too firm, nor should it be limp like a fish. If the interviewer does not extend his or her hand to you before or after the interview (this is rare), you can either make the first gesture by extending your hand or not shake hands at all.

- **Do not accept a drink within five minutes of your interview time.** You don't want to be burdened with a hot drink just as your interviewer arrives.

- Keep calm and keep your cool even if you are kept waiting. It can help to take a book or magazine to look at.

- Leave your overcoat, briefcase, umbrella, etc., in reception so you don't need to worry where to put them.

- **Be in a positive frame of mind.** You may or may not feel confident but for the interview, you must portray a positive image. There's some research that says smiling can help make you feel happy. So put on a big smile and keep your eyes smiling afterwards.

At the interview

Stand out! Be Confident! Enjoy it!

Go into every interview prepared for a rigorous questioning session, even if you have been told something like, *"We'd like you to see so-and-so; it's just a formality."* Remember 'so-and-so' can still pull the plug at any time.

> No interview is a formality.
>
> **REMEMBER**

Many interviewers make up their minds about a candidate within seconds of meeting them. This is known as the 'halo effect'. When we observe one good thing about someone, we assume all kinds of other good things about the person. It's not fair, but we do it anyway. For example, if you are well dressed, many interviewers will assume you are probably responsible in other ways.

> You only have one chance to make a first impression.
>
> **REMEMBER**

The importance of a first impression lies in the fact that, once it is made, the interviewer subconsciously wishes to have that initial favourable impression confirmed by the subsequent discussion. The opposite is the 'horns effect'. If you start off badly, perhaps by the way you are dressed, your clammy hands or tripping up as you go into the interview room, you'll have an uphill struggle for the rest of the interview.

Don't sit until you are invited to do so. If you are placed in an awkward position, ask, *"Would you mind if I moved my chair?"* and move it immediately.

> Take a few deep breaths, relax and be natural.

This is your opportunity to show the interviewer that you are the person they are looking for. Sit well back in your chair, in an upright but comfortable position. If you use your hands when talking be aware of it and don't over do it. Make friendly eye contact with the person asking questions, but don't stare.

Be friendly, confident and articulate. This means standing, sitting and walking with good posture and confidence. Grasp the interviewer's hand in a firm and decisive handshake. Call the interviewer by his or her name, saying how pleased you are to be there.

Expect to get on with your interviewer, and show you do through your verbal and non-verbal behaviour. Don't let preconceived notions about them show in your face or how you speak.

Speak loudly and clearly enough to be heard. Make sure you stress your good points, showing how well informed you are about the company. Keep your attitude businesslike and respectful. Sell yourself by giving solid reasons why you want to work for the company and how you can help them.

Make sure you recount things in an interesting and positive way so that the interviewer will remember you.

Listen closely as the interviewers introduce themselves. You will want to address them by name at some point during the interview.

If you feel uncomfortable holding eye contact with people, look at their forehead, just above their nose. If there is more than one interviewer, make sure you also involve them by addressing the next part of your answer to them. For panel interviews, address the main body of an answer to the questioner, but then hold eye contact with other panel members in order to involve them.

Be natural, relaxed and enthusiastic. Remember you are already more than half-way to the job. You are at interview because the selectors consider you **can** do the job. Unless you're a professional actor/actress, most employers will be able to see through any 'mask' you're trying to project. Be self-assured, but not over-confident, over-bearing, or arrogant. Show your passion. If there are two equally qualified candidates, the passionate one will likely get the job.

Think before you talk. Take a few seconds to collect and organise your thoughts, and then answer each question simply and directly. If you do not understand the question or the motivation behind it, ask for clarification. Use jargon or technical terms only if you fully understand them and if they will help show your knowledge of a subject. You should say this, wherever relevant, before you start to answer a question: *"Now I need to answer that question in a way that will show how I can be of value to this employer."* If you start to ramble, interrupt yourself by coughing or pausing. This will give you time to collect your thoughts and you can say *"Sorry, can I start that answer again?"*

As you cover them at interview, mentally tick off the five or six key reasons why you should be considered for the job. Find opportunities to raise any topics which have not been covered. You might be asked whether you would like to add anything or you might make the point yourself: *"Would it be helpful if I mentioned something else relevant to this job?"* Take every opportunity to explain your achievements and abilities within the context of the job description.

Never hesitate to ask the interviewer to repeat the question if you haven't fully heard or understood it. You can also use the technique of restating the question in different words to check your understanding.

Let the interviewer control the interview, but always be prepared to take the initiative. Have a strategy for handling interviewers who monopolise the talking, or ask only closed ('Yes/No') questions. Be prepared for the deliberate question which the interviewer knows you cannot answer. Such questions are useful to interviewers as much to see how you will cope as for the content of your reply.

If the interviewer starts asking the *"How would you handle...?"* questions, pretend that you are not being interviewed for a job. Instead, imagine that you are a respected consultant helping a new client with a problem. Adopt a probing approach so that you can understand their situation in sufficient detail before providing an answer. Relate your answer to their business objectives rather than to theories or models (unless specifically asked to do so).

Similarly, when asked about your past achievements, relate them to issues your employer was trying to address and the business (organisational) benefits they gained. This way, you will be giving very useful examples, and, by not trying to 'perform', you will be more relaxed.

Remember:

Keep on your toes. Everyone feels nervous before an interview; this is quite natural. Butterflies in the stomach are caused by the same surge of adrenaline that an athlete gets before an important race. It's the body's way of tuning up your faculties for peak performance. Channel this energy by keeping super-alert and notice the interviewer(s) body language for clues on how much detail you should be giving them. For example, are they attentive or bored?

Build rapport. The interview is also about what you are like to work with. Hence, building rapport may be as important as impressing with expertise.

Think! Give careful consideration to all your answers. Don't be afraid to pause and think before replying to a question, and don't hesitate to say you don't know if that is the case.

Be natural. Wanting to give your best doesn't mean that you have to be unnatural. High anxiety about the outcome can lead to candidates either trying too hard or coming over as dull and stilted. Aim to strike a balance between being (a)comfortable and relaxed and (b) alert and incisive. Above all, show your interest by your natural enthusiasm for that winning future combination – you and the job.

Be positive: Handle mistakes properly. Don't criticise previous employers as you'll project a negative image of yourself. On the other hand, if you have made a mistake in your career, it is not a disaster to admit it, but make sure you convey clearly the lessons it taught you. Admitting the odd mistake also gives you credibility when you start to talk about the positive things in your career.

IF THINGS GO WRONG

It may have been a long time since your last interview. Be prepared for anything! Plan now for what you will do if the worst happens. Such as:

You arrive late: The situation is perhaps retrievable if you apologise and offer to come back another time. No matter how late you are, do not park in the chairman's parking space and rush into the building.

You are kept waiting for a long time: Do not complain. Check regularly with reception, and if offered a replacement interview, accept it.

You can't remember the interviewer's name: Ask the receptionist. On no account should you admit your oversight.

You spill your tea or coffee: If you have interview nerves, don't accept a drink. Should you find yourself in such a dilemma, however, do clean it up.

The interview is regularly interrupted: Offer to leave the room or to come back at another time.

Your mind goes blank: This usually occurs when people are extremely nervous. If it happens, take a couple of deep breaths, (which will calm you down by getting oxygen to your brain), and try to get your perspective again.

You can stall for time saying something like, *"I couldn't quite hear you exactly, could you repeat that?"* Or you could tell the truth and say *"I'm sorry, my mind has gone blank."* You could then explain that you are prone to nerves in interviews and your disarming honesty may save the day (unless you are applying for a job that requires you to keep your nerves, such as a fire-fighter).

You are asked a question you don't know the answer to: If the question is a factual one and you don't know, then admit this with a smile and explain that this particular question is outside of your experience. If the question is a theoretical one, ask for a few moments to collect your thoughts so that you can give a considered answer. Preface any answer with *"I'm not sure if this is exactly what you are asking, but..."*

You are interviewed in a noisy and crowded room: This is a sign of an inexperienced interviewer who may be trying to suggest that he is so important that he cannot leave the centre of his powerhouse. In most cases, you will just have to put up with it and concentrate hard to keep out the interruptions. Follow up with a letter to confirm key points or clarify areas you missed.

The question doesn't make sense: Ask them to repeat or rephrase the questions. If you misunderstand a question your interviewer may assume that you are a bit dim.

If you get some bad news on the day of the interview: The best solution may be to ring beforehand, explain the situation and see if another appointment can be found.

You don't like your interviewer: Don't let it put you off if you really want the job. Try to 'like' them as much as possible during the interview, because such feelings can communicate themselves through body language. After the interview, you may like to reflect if you would want to join the company, particularly if you will be working closely with the interviewer.

You know your interviewer: Don't let this worry you. If it is a one-to-one, the interviewer may need to consider their position and the onus would be on them to do something about it. If there is more than one person interviewing you, your contact is under less pressure.

POST-INTERVIEW EVALUATION

Once you are out of the building, and in your car, at the train station, etc., jot down a few notes, outlining the main points discussed. Also ask yourself the following questions:

- What was the interviewer's full name and title?
- What was the receptionist/secretary's name?
- Who else from the company did you meet?
- Exactly what does the job entail?
- Did they mention salary? What was said?

As soon as you can, complete a review of how you think you came across. It will be invaluable to refer to if you get a second interview and you can also use it to monitor your performance. Be honest with yourself, noting what you did well, and where improvements are needed. Talk through the result of your review with a friend and practise your revised answers.

There are many questions you can ask yourself such as:

- Was I in the right frame of mind?

- Was my eye contact right, did I smile?

- Was there anything I should have known about the company that I did not?

- How effective was my role in the interview?

- Which questions did I handle well? Which questions did I handle poorly?

- How well did I ask questions? What could I have done differently?

- Did I appear confident and show genuine enthusiasm?

- Did I talk too much?

- Did I give answers which didn't seem to satisfy the interviewer?

- Was I able to discuss my strengths and weaknesses?

- Did I seem interested and enthusiastic about the job?

- Did I find out all I needed to?

- Would I like to work for that organisation?

A more detailed Post-Interview Evaluation Form can be downloaded from the website.

CONTACTING THE RECRUITMENT AGENCY

If you have been put forward by a recruitment agency, call them as soon as you can to let them know how you got on and to confirm your interest in the job. They will almost certainly feed this straight back to the interviewer and it will be viewed positively.

FOLLOW UP WITH A THANK-YOU LETTER

Typically, only about 25% of applicants write a follow-up letter to thank the interviewer for their time. If the interviewer is still deciding between you and another applicant, this may just tip the balance in your favour.

A follow-up letter gives you an opportunity to reinforce your strengths, and demonstrates your written communication skills. A hand-written letter shows you took the time to write it, and it doesn't come across as a standard reply you send to every interviewer. Speed of delivery is very important. If you can't get the letter there for the next day, it's better to send it by email.

Your thank-you letter can address areas of weakness, reservations or concerns that were mentioned during the interview. You can also reiterate your strengths and explain why you are the person for the job. Mention how your strengths and past work history (with examples) can over-compensate for any areas of weakness.

Structure of a thank-you letter

Paragraph 1

Thank you for interviewing me for the position of xxx on (date).

Paragraph 2

Restate what you have to offer to the company.

After discussing the responsibilities of the job, I am sure that I have the skills and experience to perform well in this position. Mention again what you can bring to the job.

Paragraph 3

Thank the interviewer. Say how you may be contacted.

Thank you again for taking the time to meet with me. If you need additional information, I can be reached at xxx in the daytime and at xxx in the evenings.

If your interview did not go well or if you want to add something that was not covered, you can use the thank-you letter as a follow-up marketing tool. Include a paragraph that makes your point and encourages the employer to reconsider your potential. A sample letter is below:

Thank you for the opportunity to interview with you last Tuesday for the position of Business Development Manager. During the interview you asked why I was a good candidate and I could only give you a vague response. I have spent time evaluating my strengths in relation to your needs. After serious consideration I can comfortably state that I am a good candidate because _____.

If you would like to discuss in more depth my background in relation to your needs, please call. Otherwise, I look forward to hearing your decision. I am still very interested in working for you at XYZ plc.

Based on your questions you might have found out about a particular problem the company or interviewer has. You can then prepare for...

Second and third interviews

> Always ask about the next steps after the interview and when you will hear from them. Then make a diary note to get in touch the day after.

You will need to do some extra research. **The more knowledgeable you are in advance, the more effective you will be.** Remember that everyone you meet from division head to support staff is evaluating you just as you are evaluating them. Don't forget to review your notes from the first interview.

YOU GET A REGRET LETTER

If you get a regret letter, *"We regret to inform you . . ."*, it could be for one of five reasons:

1. **There was not a good match between you and the job.** In this case, the rejection letter is a positive outcome. You would not have liked that job anyway.

2. **You do not have the right background for this job.** You may not yet be ready for this job. If you applied for a position as marketing manager, perhaps you should apply for a marketing executive job to gain more experience.

3. **There was a good match but you simply did not interview well.** You need to spend time on interview practice.

4. **The applicant pool was extremely competitive.** There may have been more than one person who was capable of doing the job. The final decision may have been based on factors outside your control. The person who got the job may have been an internal candidate or had something extra to offer.

5. **There is no job available.** This could be because the head office wants to fill the vacancy but the local branch has no intention of filling it, or the job has already been offered to someone, and the ad was to 'go through the motions'.

Whatever you think is the reason you didn't get the job, contact the company and ask them for feedback.

Finally, even if you do not get an offer, you can still write one last letter. The person who has been offered the job may turn it down and this could lead to an offer for you. Plus, it will definitely leave a favourable impression.

A reply to the regret letter

Quite regularly, a new employee leaves quite quickly as it hasn't worked out for them. Your reply could bring you to the top of the list when a new person is being considered.

> *Thank you for your kind call to tell me that the Business Improvement Manager vacancy has been filled. Although I was not selected for the position, I want to wish you and the new manager well as you begin to work together.*
>
> *Once again, thank you for the consideration you have given my application for this position. As your personnel requirements change in the future, I hope you will keep me in mind and contact me.*

You could also ask for feedback on how you missed out so you can give some attention to the reason you were not chosen.

YOU'VE GOT THE JOB!

If you get a job offer, you will want to consider whether it is the right job for you, and then to negotiate the salary and benefits package.

Of course, you may decide to turn an offer down. If you do, do so quickly and send a letter which keeps the possibility of your getting in touch again in the future. For example:

> *Thank you for offering me a position as a Marketing Executive with Guardian Consulting. I found our discussions during the interview process very enlightening as to the details of this position, and I appreciate the time you allowed me to consider your offer. I was also able to confirm my initial impressions of Guardian Consulting as an outstanding organisation.*

However, after considerable thought about my career goals, I'm afraid I must respectfully decline your kind offer. I have chosen to accept an offer from an employer based closer to my home. This was a difficult decision for me, although I believe it is the appropriate one at this point in my career.

I want to thank you for the time and consideration you have given my application. It was a pleasure meeting you and learning more about Guardian Consulting.

Visit the website to download the additional resources:

- *Post-Interview Evaluation Form*

Chapter Twenty

PSYCHOMETRIC TESTING

Many companies seek to make the selection of candidates more rigorous by the use of a process known as an 'assessment centre', which involves an extended range of interviews and testing. Ability tests are often used to reduce the number of applicants to form a shortlist. Sometimes psychometric tests are the first part of an assessment centre. There are two main types: tests of ability and personality questionnaires.

Ability tests include verbal reasoning, critical thinking, numerical reasoning and spatial skills. Each test question has a right and wrong answer.

Personality questionnaires include Saville's Wave, 16PF5, and the OPQ (Occupational Personality Questionnaire). They seek to understand the sort of person you are, and your responses will be followed up with a detailed interview with a psychologist or psychometrician.

Can you prepare for tests?

It's difficult to prepare for a test when you don't know the content of the questions. However, you can practise technique that will make you feel more confident. There are numerous books containing practice material and it's also possible to access example tests through the Internet.

For numerical tests, you will often need to be able to calculate percentages and deal with ratios. You may want to practise doing these calculations to ensure you can do them on the day of the test.

Will I get details of tests when I apply for a job?

If you apply for a job and you are invited to a test session, you should receive details of the tests and some practice information. If not, ask, as it's good policy for employers to provide it.

Can I fail a test?

Tests are not thought of as pass/fail as the scores are usually presented as percentiles. So a score at the 60th percentile, for example, does not mean a score of 60%. It means you scored better than 60% of a comparable group.

You cannot 'fail' a personality questionnaire and you should always be given an opportunity to discuss your results with a qualified assessor. This will enable you to provide examples to support the responses you gave.

Preparation for an ability testing session

There are things you can do to improve your performance in psychometric tests, such as:

- Reading newspapers, reports and business journals to improve your verbal skills for verbal tests.

- Reading financial reports in newspapers, studying tables of data, doing number calculations and puzzles without a calculator may help numerical skills.

- Checking results in the paper could improve checking skills.

- Solving crosswords may help verbal problem solving.

- Looking at objects in various ways and angles could develop spatial skills.

- Looking at flow charts and diagrams should improve diagramming skills.

There are also many books with sample tests you can practise in advance including my book *Now you've been shortlisted*. Such practice can help you prepare.

The night before the test

The best thing to do is get a good night's sleep and try to relax.

During the ability testing session

- Keep as calm as you can. Remember that a certain amount of anxiety is perfectly normal.

- Make sure that you are comfortable. Loosen your collar and tie (if appropriate), and kick off your shoes if you want.

- Listen carefully to the administrator's instructions. Ask questions if you need to.

- If you can't see or hear things properly, tell the administrator.

- Read the test instructions carefully and do not assume that you know what to do.

- Put your answers in the right place on the answer sheet! (It's easy to make mistakes in the heat of the moment.)

- Record your answers in the correct way. For example, do not tick boxes if you're expected to strike through them with short pencil lines.

- Read the questions properly before you attempt to answer them.

- Don't agonise over a question you can't answer – move on to the next one.

- Don't waste time double checking questions with easy or obvious answers.

- Don't waste time looking for 'trick questions', as there won't be any.

- If you can't work out an answer, make an informed guess.

- Work as quickly as you can, but don't race or you will make avoidable mistakes.

- Remember that the more questions you answer, the greater your chances of getting a higher mark.

- With some questions, a good approach can be to eliminate the wrong answers to arrive at the correct one. It's often better to guess, rather than to leave a question unanswered, but do check to make sure you will not be penalised for incorrect answers.

- Keep an eye on the time. If you have time left at the end of a test go back and check your answers.

- Don't stick to a certain amount of time for each question. Many tests are designed so that the questions get harder, and you'll need more time as you progress.

- Look around occasionally and take some deep breaths, it will help you relax.

- Don't be put off if the questions seem difficult, they may well be just as difficult for everybody else.

- Avoid extreme reactions. Take the test confidently and purposefully and avoid being too blasé, because some tests will discriminate between the able and the extremely able.

- Some tests will place greater emphasis on accuracy and others on the number of questions attempted – always ask for clarification before you begin.

- Don't be alarmed if other people appear to be working more quickly. It doesn't mean that they are getting the answers right!

Personality testing is a bit different. There will be no right or wrong answers and you will not have to worry about how to deal with complex tasks. Instead, you will be asked questions and the results will be used to determine the sort of person you are.

It can be tempting to want to portray yourself in the most positive light, but tests come with scales that will pick up if you are overly lenient or critical in your responses. You may also decide to pretend that you are, for example, more outgoing than you actually are, or more strategic. However, the assessment will be followed by a discussion, and if you don't have the examples to support what you say, it can put a cloud of 'who is he/she really' over the whole results; or if you are a good actor you may end up in a job that's a poor match to your personality.

Chapter Twenty One

ASSESSMENT CENTRES

When you apply for a job, the potential employer's decision may be based on more than an interview. You may need to take part in an assessment centre. This is a much more detailed and time-consuming way of deciding on the right person for the job.

An assessment centre consists of a number of different exercises and interviews. Some people excel at interviews, but not everyone. Being able to undertake different exercises gives you greater opportunities to demonstrate your strengths and abilities.

> Before the centre, you need to prepare.

Read the company literature

You should be sent details of the competencies that are to be used in the assessment centre. These will all be assessed. So if, for example, strategic understanding is one of the competencies measured in the test, you will want to make sure you think strategically. If a certain competency doesn't come naturally to you, take some time to prepare, both for questioning and written work.

Ask for a copy of the timetable, if not supplied, so you understand what the day will consist of.

Make sure you know where the venue is and arrive in plenty of time, allowing time for delays in transport. Get a good night's sleep the night before, and take your reading glasses with you. Along with your CV and copy of the application form, take a set of highlighter pens. If there is written work, a highlighter is a great way of emphasising key words and facts.

On the day

On arrival, you will meet the centre manager who should talk you through the day. You will also meet your fellow candidates. In most cases, this will be a competitive assessment centre, but you should be pleasant and make general conversation. Some candidates may want to play 'mind games' and talk up their experience and background.

Don't be taken in and overawed by what other people say. It's your performance on the day that counts. In many cases there is no 'winner' at an assessment centre, i.e. you are not in a competition with the other candidates – all of you, or none of you, may be offered a position.

Assessment centres will sometimes start with a group introduction and move onto a group exercise, whereas assessment centres at a senior level may keep candidates apart.

Generally, a timetable will allow time for breaks. But sometimes you are given all the day's activities to do at the beginning and it's up to you to manage your time. If this is the case, listen carefully for any clues the centre manager may give you. Be aware that you might be called for an interview part of the way through a task. Some centres do this to see how well you cope with this sort of interruption.

The group exercise

Group exercises are used to see how you relate to others. Usually, you will be given information to read in advance, and then join with others for the discussion. Everyone has an objective of achieving a personal task, but you also need to consider the overall group and not alienate others. Generally, there is no right answer in a group exercise; how you reach an answer while working in your group is more important.

You must speak up and speak clearly so the assessors can hear you. No matter how shy you are, and how much you prefer to think about things before speaking, in a group exercise you must speak up so the assessors have something to assess. Someone in the group needs to structure the task and the time, so if no one else takes on this role, you may volunteer. However, don't volunteer to keep track of the time unless you are sure you will!

It always helps to address people by name. All the people in your group should be wearing name badges, but if not, as everyone introduces themselves at the beginning, note their name (possibly using a diagram which you can refer to). As you are likely to be assessed on your ability to get on with others, refrain from talking too much.

You may like to encourage contributions from a quieter person to show your awareness of the importance of teamwork.

Keep track of the time so you can suggest when it would be good to move on. Make sure to save some time at the end for summarising.

In tray exercise

You will be given a number of documents and will need to make a judgement on what to do within the time allowed. The scenario is usually that your boss is unavailable, it's your first day, and you need to go through a series of papers in a limited amount of time before a meeting. There is often a connection between documents, so read them through quickly. You may want to delegate tasks to other people. If you do, provide clear instructions.

Be sure to say thank you and refer to people by name.

The written exercise

Some organisations may give you a lot of material and a short amount of time to grasp the key points and respond to a task. Review this information, quickly make sense of it, then produce a report. Read through the instructions carefully. If you are asked to refer to specific criteria, make sure you do. If it asks for a recommendation, make one and justify your choice. Written skills are likely to be assessed so take care about spelling, grammar and layout. The use of paragraphs, headers and sub headings can help the reader. Often, you will notice numerical data in the material available and doing calculations is likely to impress the assessor and score extra points!

Presentations

Some assessment centres send material in advance so you can prepare your presentation beforehand. In this case, a very high standard is expected as you will have time to prepare visual aids and practice your talk. Other centres give you a limited amount of time to prepare on the day and thus, you do not have to reach such a high standard (but you still need to appear competent).

When presenting, make eye contact with the assessor(s) and have a clear start and end to your thoughts. This will provide a positive impression and make it clear to the assessors that they can move into the questioning phase.

After your presentation, you will be asked questions.

Expect to be challenged on what you have said and when questioned, take a moment or two to think through how best to reply. A measured response that is focused on the question is more effective than a rambling reply.

Interviews

The key is to be prepared. You will be aware of the competences, so think of examples that demonstrate yours. If you know you are going to be asked questions about relationships, think through examples in both your working and non work life. For example, think about when you have worked successfully with others, when there have been tension and conflicts and then think through how you dealt (or will deal) with these.

Often you will be asked questions to ascertain resilience.

Think about pressure situations, how you dealt with them, and what you learned from them. Don't think you have to come across as superman or superwoman – it can be valuable to discuss what may have gone wrong and what you have learned from specific situations.

Different companies can have slightly different definitions of the same competency, so carefully read the information that is provided. Break down the details and think through examples of each aspect.

Don't forget to re-read Chapter 18, Interview preparation and Chapter 19, The interview – you're shortlisted! to remind you about interviews.

Treat each exercise separately

We're not always the best judge of our own performance. The best way to approach assessment centres is to treat each element independently, whether you think you have done fantastically well, or very badly. Then leave the exercise and move onto the next one in a positive manner.

I once interviewed someone who spent 10 minutes telling me what a hash they had made of their written exercise. In my interview, they struggled to keep focused and I think their thoughts on the previous exercise were still prominent in their mind. Later, I found out their written script was fine, but they did poorly in my session, and they were not offered a job.

Conclusion

Assessment centres can be stressful, but they are also a good opportunity for you to demonstrate your strengths in a number of areas. As well as the company learning quite a lot about you, you will also learn more about the job you are seeking. If an assessment centre exercise asks you to analyse complex data, this is likely to be a component of the job.

Most organisations will provide you with some feedback on your performance, sometimes verbal and at other times, a full report. Sometimes it is sent to everyone, sometimes you need to request it, so make sure you contact the company. It is good practice for companies to do this, and you can review the feedback to help you in the future.

Section 7
Keeping Going

This final section will help you to stay motivated and review progress. Once you get the job offer, use Chapter 23 to ensure you have considered everything before you say yes. Finally, read about all the additional resources available via a simple signup online.

Chapter Twenty Two

STAYING MOTIVATED

No matter how positive a person you are, it may prove challenging to stay motivated in the current economic climate. With news of companies closing down every day and more and more people seeking a job, you may wonder if there will ever be a job for you. What the newspapers ignore are the number of jobs that are still being advertised each day. There are jobs out there, and staying motivated will help you find one that's right for you.

FOLLOW A DAILY PLAN

Motivation is helped by a daily plan and reviewing each day what you have done that worked and what else you could do. This book has provided you with the plan, so are you following it? We can often think we are doing the right things, but over the weeks we deviate and get a little off-plan, so it can help to re-read what to do and reenergise yourself. If you need more help, sign up for the 21-day eProgramme.

AVOID THE NEGATIVE SELF TALK

Negative self-talk can really hamper our chance of a new job. If we ask ourselves, *"Why can't I get a job?"* our brains will focus on all the reasons why we can't get one – we are too old or too young, too fat or too short, have too much experience or not enough.

We need to change focus and ask a better question. Good questions to ask include:

- What can I do to get this job?

- How can I show an employer that I'm the right person for this job?

This gets you thinking of specific examples such as putting a monetary value on your achievements, creating a portfolio of your work, and more. Re-read Chapter 16 to remind yourself of other things to do.

Don't let negative thoughts get you down

It's easy to feel down when a job offer does not appear. You may find yourself lamenting that *"I have to complete another application form,"* or *"I've got to revise my CV."* But don't make it seem like it's such a chore. Gather yourself and try to think positively and set out to enjoy the task. You could set yourself the challenge of completing it to a high standard in a set time then give yourself a treat afterwards.

It's too easy to let negative thoughts come into our heads. You know, the things like:

- I'm too young or too old.
- I can't afford it.
- I'm scared.
- I don't know where to start.
- I don't have enough time.
- People will think I'm mad.
- People will be jealous if I succeed.
- What if I fail?
- I'm not smart enough.
- I don't have the energy to do this.

But why not turn them around? For example:

"I'm not too young/old, but I'm the perfect age to get started".

Instead of worrying about not knowing where to start, say: *"I'm ready to get started"*, and let your subconscious work on this. Use external help if needed such as from a coach or friend.

If you expect to be unsuccessful in meetings and at interview, then you are likely to come across that way, and you'll be seen as someone who can't confidently discuss the great examples of their experience. On the other hand, if you think you are going to be successful and have planned how to respond to questions and ask questions, you stand a much better chance.

DEALING WITH REJECTION

You will get set backs and knock backs. No matter how great your application, you may still not get to interview. Some companies have literally hundreds of applications and have no time to review them all. In those cases, it's really a matter of luck if your CV is reviewed at all!

You may think you have a great CV, but if it is not getting you to interview, it's not doing its job. So keep track of your rejection letters, and if necessary, seek an independent job-search coach to provide feedback and guidance to help you improve.

It may be that you need to create a more focused CV and cover letter, or you may need to spend more time on research.

In the same sense, you may think you interview well, but carrying out a full interview with an experienced interviewer who coaches you is worth the investment. The relevant chapters in this book tell you how to conduct yourself at interview, and your practice sessions with a friend may help you improve, but you may still benefit from exploring other subtleties with an experienced interviewer.

The impact on others

Feel sorry for yourself and you will feel like a victim; spend too much time moaning and people won't want to be around you. Look for ways to remain interesting and to keep friendships and relationships going.

Keep a positive attitude

"Whether you think you can or you can't, you're right." – Henry Ford

You need a positive attitude; you need to believe that you can do something, that you can achieve your goal. You could find inspiration through books and reading other peoples success stories. Join the Facebook group AmazingPeopleUK to share good news and get energised and inspired through reading what others have done. Would it help to create a mantra? Have something you can repeat to keep you going through the day.

Remind yourself of previous successes

Do you remember the time you won a race, created a great report, made a presentation that convinced your boss to go ahead with a project or to give you a rise? Now is the time to remind yourself of previous successes. You might like to buy a small notebook and write them down as you remember them. You've been successful before and you will be again.

Visualise yourself succeeding

Why not imagine yourself being successful in your job search? It can be a very powerful technique. Think of how you will dress and what the workplace will be like. Imagine yourself at your desk and on the phone, talking with customers or in the field delivering goods and services.

Maybe the image isn't clear at the moment, but try and picture yourself carrying out your ideal job – what will you be wearing? How will you be feeling? What will you be doing?

Successful athletes dream about winning. They visualise themselves achieving their goal. You can do the same! Each evening when you go to bed, make a movie in your head of being in your ideal job. What do you see? What can you hear? What can you taste or smell? Notice how great you feel! Run this movie through your head again – make it bigger, brighter, and sharper.

You might get there sooner than you think!

Remind yourself that it's not all within your control

> Don't internalise positive and negative events. Not getting a job does not mean that you are not a wonderful person; the rejection is not personal.

You can have a great CV, interview well, and look great, but still find yourself unemployed and waiting for a job offer. With the recession, there are many people in exactly your position. So keep doing the best you can and don't take your lack of a job offer too personally.

Do you spend too much time watching the news?

If each day you watch programmes about how awful the job market is, how many people are being made redundant etc, you may wonder how you will ever find a job yourself. Remember, you are not trying to get a job for everyone – just one job, for you.

Does your family get you down?

Are your partner or parents continually asking you when you are going to get a job? One way to keep them 'off your back' is to set up a weekly review time so you can show what you have done and what you plan to do for the subsequent week. Tell them how their nagging isn't helping, and recruit them to be part of your network, assisting you in finding leads and people to talk with.

Are your friends helping?

Some people love to be negative, to see the world as a half-empty glass, to complain, to see problems, to expect to fail. Spend too much time with people like this and you are likely to start thinking the same way. Who do you know that will inspire you and keep you feeling positive? You need to spend more time with people like that! Perhaps you should look to broaden the circle of people you know and meet more positive people. Perhaps joining a book group or a walking group would help. Find out details of groups local to you through meetup.com.

WHEN YOUR JOB SEARCH HAS STALLED

Has your job search stalled? Review what you have been doing

Start measuring

How many hours a day are you spending on your job search? List everything you are doing and the amount of time you spend doing each one. How much is effective job search, and how much just passes the time? It's not about the number of CVs you send out or the number of jobs you apply for but the effective action you take. It's better to do one well-thought-through application than to mail out 30 unfocused CVs.

Your job search campaign

Each week, review what you have done and what you will do next week – what is working and what is not? If something isn't working, try it again and then try something new.

Is there anything that you are avoiding? Make a note and ask others to help you get past this block. There are many things you could measure, for example:

- How many jobs have you applied for?

- Do you know the companies you want to work for?

- Are you following every company you want to work for on FaceBook, LinkedIn, Twitter?

- How many interviews have you had?

- How many phone calls have you made?

- How many jobs do you think you are a great match with?

- How many contacts have you connected with this week?

- How many people have you *reconnected* with?

- How many people have you connected with on LinkedIn this week?

- How many direct approaches have you made?

- How many professional meetings have you attended?

PLUS make sure that you can say yes to the following:

- Do you have an email signature?

- Is your LinkedIn profile 100% complete?

- Do you have more than 100 contacts on LinkedIn?

- Do you share links and updates with 10% of your contact list?

- Do you have a personal website or blog?

- Are you using Twitter to follow key people within the companies you want to work for?

Do review everything. Is your CV as good as can be? Could you improve your interview techniques?

Research

For the job you seek, will there be jobs available soon, or are the jobs unlikely to be available? Stop chasing jobs that have gone and look for jobs that are available, and ideally in a growing market.

> Look to celebrate mini achievements, such as a trip to the cinema after 20 cold-calls.

Are you doing fact-finding interviews?

Could you be finding out more about the industry or company you want to work for?

Are you relying too much on other people?

Are you waiting for people to get back to you? Nobody has your interests as high a priority as you do. You have to take charge and keep focused. Posting your CV on job sites and waiting for recruitment consultants is not enough. Don't just read but *follow* the advice in this book!

Are you taking no as no?

Don't give up. Sales people know it can take seven attempts to make a sale, and no doesn't mean no for ever, just not right now. You can approach a company again.

Keep making changes

On job search boards, make a minor change several times a week to keep your details at the top of the search list.

Quit, just for a while

If what you are doing isn't working, why not quit? Give yourself a job search holiday. Take some time out and take your CV down from all the job sites. Have someone undertake a critical review of your CV. From a read-through is it clear what you want? Then start afresh.

Think of the upside

You will have more free time, so use some of it to do something you have never had time to do before, such as learning the tin whistle or a language, or getting fitter with a daily run. Plus, if you never really enjoyed your last job, it does give you time to find a job you love (or at least like better than the last one).

Develop new skills

Learn something that will enhance your CV, it doesn't have to be an expensive course; there are lots of training opportunities available for free. For example, you can access online training via the **Massachusetts Institute of Technology online site** at http://ocw. mit.edu. You may not be able to gain a qualification but you can still learn new skills.

> How can you improve – what can you do today to make a difference?

Get a job search buddy

It can be hard work, searching for a job alone, so find a buddy and meet on a weekly basis to share progress. You can both encourage each other, or post what you have done on the Amazing People Facebook page and follow what others are sharing.

Be helpful – volunteer

If you do have spare time, why not do some voluntary work? This could be using the skills you already have to benefit others, or it may be an opportunity to develop some new skills. In many volunteer positions, you will be dealing with people who have problems, and this will make you more grateful for what you have. It can also mean that you may meet people in a position to offer you a job. At the very least, you will definitely meet new people who you can add to your network. And remember, volunteer work looks great on a CV, and many prospective employers think highly of a person who is involved with volunteer activities.

The best volunteering is to do something related to the job you seek. If you are a marketing executive, offer to create a marketing plan for a charity. This will be far more effective for your job search than volunteering to work in a charity shop or tidying a country park.

Connect with more people

Of course you will be talking with people who have a high probability of helping you reach your job-hunting goals but sometimes you may find that talking with neighbours and spending time listening to them are helpful in both building your community and directing you to the right contacts.

Take some time to have fun

Job search doesn't have to be a 12-hour-a-day job. Spending four hours directly on your job search allows you time to develop some research and interview skills, and still leave time for friends and relaxation.

Chapter Twenty Three

BEFORE YOU SAY YES

If you are unemployed, and the recession brings up concerns about when you will get another job, you may want to say yes to any job offer. But wait. Make sure that it's the right job for you. After examining things, you may still go ahead and take it, but you will do so with more realistic expectations.

Just because you get an offer doesn't mean you should say yes. Your interview can be a good indicator of how you are going to be treated in the job. Kim was extremely pleased to be shortlisted for a job with a professional law firm with impressive offices. The interview with the HR manager went well but when she met her potential boss, it was awful.

If you were treated badly at or you hear people making negative comments about the company, think twice before saying yes. One of the worst things you can do is take a job and within a couple of weeks realise you made the wrong choice. You then have to spend time learning the current new job, leaving even less time for a new job search. Or you may resign and have a problem explaining to a new employer why you left so quickly.

So, before you say yes:

Send a letter to show your enthusiasm for the job. This letter should summarise your strengths, and outline your key accomplishments and personal contributions.

Remind them why they have chosen you. If the employer's compensation package is included in the letter, say how excited you are and that you would like a couple of days to discuss things with your partner. This gives you a chance to weigh the pros and cons of the job, and to get in touch with any other companies to which you have applied to check how your applications are progressing.

Make sure it hits all the right buttons

Check the job offer against your key criteria. How well does it match up?

Gill was one of a number of clients who was seduced into thinking the job was perfect for her. She was going to be marketing manager for an international company and would be meeting with colleagues from around the world on a regular basis. The job was quite a stretch for her but she convinced herself she was up to the challenge. After all, the pay was going to be 30% more than she was currently making and she was being offered a BMW as a company car. Who wouldn't take such a job?

Gill contacted me and she came across as very excited and positive about this new job. She looked at me a bit strange when I asked her what was really important to her in her new job, then she listed all the benefits she would gain – the car, the travel, the status.

How important is that I asked? Again she looked at me a bit surprised. I could tell she was confused as to why I was asking these questions, so I explained the importance of career satisfaction to overall well-being and that it would help if we took some time to define what characteristics would bring her satisfaction at work.

I did the following exercise with her. She was to rate the importance of each on a scale of 1–10.

WHAT IS IMPORTANT TO YOU IN A JOB?

Security. If you have been made redundant, you may be looking for a job with a secure company.

Salary. How well can I live on the salary that has been offered? Is it commission only? Does it include profit share?

Work content. Does the job sound interesting and challenging?

Working environment. Will I look forward to going to work each day?

Travel time. Will I be happy to do this in deepest winter? How far will I have to commute, and realistically how long will the journey take?

Benefits. Is the package acceptable? What does it consist of? Could I get more?

Promotion prospects. Will I have an opportunity to move forward in this company? Will it help my future career prospects with another company?

Security. Is the company likely to go out of business?

Friendly atmosphere. Do I fit in with the company culture?

Prestigious company. How well respected in the community is the company?

Contributes to defined career path. How well does this job fit in with my long-range career goals?

Hours. Will I mind working the hours required for success in this job? Will I be happy to work unsociable hours? How important is it for me to spend time with my family?

Colleagues and client group. Will I want to work with people like this?

Do I really want this job? Does the work interest me?

When you get a job offer, answering these questions enables you to take a much more objective view of decision making. These questions also allow you to choose between options, weighing each against the other.

For Gill, comparing this job offer with her ideal job of working as a charity fundraiser didn't match up. So why was she considering it? Because she was letting the money and overseas travel influence her even though they were not high on her list of important aspects of career satisfaction.

Your challenge: be clear about what you want from a job so you can make an informed decision when offered a position.

Before saying yes, ask yourself

- Will this job make good use of my abilities, skills and talents?

- Does it suit my personality?

- Am I happy that I will be paid fairly for the work I'll do?

- Does the working environment suit my values and personal preferences?

- Will it give me a chance to develop and grow?

- Does my manager have the right approach to bring out the best in me?

- What impact will taking this job have on my personal and family life?

- Are the expectations on me realistic and achievable?

- Why specifically do I want to take this job?

- And how well does it match my ideal job?

Finalise the details

Before saying yes, make sure you also know the answers to these questions:

Job title

- To whom do I report? Can I meet the person?

- Who will report to me?

- Am I clear on the duties expected of me? Do I have a full copy of the job description?

- Are the limits of my authority clearly defined?

276

Hours of work

- What are the hours of work?

- What are the sick pay entitlements?

- What are the holiday entitlements?

- Will any pre-booked holidays be honoured?

- How long will it take me to get to work and back each day at rush hour, and how much will this cost?

Meet people in the company

Arrange to talk with other employees to get an inside perspective. This could be your new manager and colleagues, or recent graduates of a management training course.

Saying no

Some people will think it foolish to turn down a job, especially in the current economic climate, but if it isn't providing what is important to you (you are being asked to work too many hours, thus creating a very low hourly wage, or you're not sure you'll enjoy the work as much as you'd like), then you may be better off waiting for a job that's more appealing.

But make sure you have considered everything the job offers, including the salary. For you, it may be better to get 75% of what you ideally want than continue for another six months being unemployed.

If you do decide to turn the job down, do so politely.

Show your appreciation for their interest and express regret that you cannot accept the offer. Remember, you may be considering employment with these people again in a few years, and you want to leave the door open for future possibilities.

Further Information

You can access a wide range of additional resources from the website at www.HowToGetAJobInARecession.com

There are

- Extensive range of forms to use including
    - Daily activity log
    - Weekly review
    - Networking record sheet

- Helpful handouts including
    - Competency questions and answers
    - Fact-finding summary
    - Post-interview feedback
    - Mock interview handout

- Audio tracks to download to your MP3 player or to listen to online including
    - How to get the best from a formal networking event
    - Career assessments
    - Appearance and body language

- Links to useful websites for ease of access

- Links to the AmazingPeople Facebook page to share ideas and ask questions.

You can also sign up for the 21-day eProgramme and receive an email each day to keep you focused.

One of the top UK career strategists, Denise Taylor specialises in career and job search coaching. She is the founder of Amazing People, a double-award-winning career-coaching company. Denise is a chartered psychologist, Associate Fellow of the British Psychological Society and an Advanced Registered Guidance Practitioner.

Many people offer career coaching, what has made Denise stand out for over 25 years is how she uses her energy and creativity to identify new trends and advanced techniques that keep her clients at the frontier. It's not enough to learn new ways of advancing your career though; you need the determination to turn it into consistent action.

Denise's other books include *Now You've Been Shortlisted*; *Winning Interview Answers for First-time Job Hunters*; and the eBook, *How To Use LinkedIn To Find A New Job*. Denise is regularly featured as an expert in the media including *The Times, The Sun, She, Top Santé, Esquire, Metro, Daily Mail,* and *The Guardian Career Forums*.

Meet Denise online at

www.amazingpeople.co.uk
www.facebook.com/amazingpeopleUK
www.howtogetajobinarecession.com
http://twitter.com/amazingpeople